FOREVERHOPEFUL

JUDITH
&
PAUL E. VANDER WEGE

ISBN: 9798869383822

This book is dedicated to my wife, Judith Vander Wege,

who is an encouragement, support, critic and all around
wonderful wife to me.

I am so blessed that she is mine.

God bless you, Sweetie.

Table of Contents

Forever Hopeful

Chapter One

"I'm going to the ball field," Lynn said. "Why?" Tony asked, riding his

bicycle up close behind Lynn's.
"You can't hit the ball. You who are blind in one eye always strike out. Besides, we don't want fellows with strange names playing with us."

"I've just as much right to play ball here in River Valley, Iowa as you do," said Lynn. Tony followed Lynn as they rode their bikes to the school grounds.

I wonder what the problem is with Tony today? There is nothing wrong with my name. My grandfather had the same name. I was named after him. I loved him until he died. I'm proud of my name.

They parked their bikes at the school. "There's a ballgame here. Maybe I'll be chosen to play."

"Who's going to choose you? You never hit the ball. You always strike out." Lynn stopped and stared at Tony with his mouth open, but no words came out.

"Don't choose Lynn," Tony shouted. The playground was full of boys and girls wanting to play ball. "Ho, ho. Hey guys, this boy wants to play, but he always strikes out. Don't choose him."

The captains chose sides ignoring Lynn. He would not be chosen again. Lynn hung his head, shuffled over to the fence behind first base and watched as the game began.

----

*I wish I could play, I'm never chosen because I'm a poor player. Tony is so good at sports; it seems he is good at all sports, but how can I improve if I don't play?*Leaning against the fence Lynn watched the game for awhile. Soon he grew tired of being ignored. *He dug* the toe of his sneakers into the dirt.   *I might as well go home.*   Lynn climbed on his bicycle and rode slowly home. *I hope Mom doesn't see me.*

"Lynn, why are you home? You said you were going to play ball," his mother said.

"I wasn't chosen to play," Lynn said.

"Why not?"

"I'm not good enough to play, I strike out every time I come to bat," Lynn said.

"That's foolishness. You go back out there and tell them I said to let you play," his mother said.

"Mom, they'll all laugh at me and call me a mommy's boy," Lynn said.

"Nonsense, now go immediately and don't argue with me!" Lynn's mother shouted.

"I'm not going Mom," Lynn said.

"I'm your Mother and I expect you to obey me. Now go!"

"Oh, all right, I'll see you later," mumbled Lynn. He rode his bike around the corner of the garage. Once out of his mother's sight, he stopped by the tool shed and took his fishing gear and tackle box. He dug some worms, peddled to the Little Sioux River, and settled on the bank to fish. He saw Bob and Susan fishing about ten feet away.

After baiting his hook he cast the line into a quiet pool nearby.

Sitting down on a large rock so he wouldn't get chigger bites, he watched the scenery around him. The trees along both sides of the river cast cool shadows over the water. The cows in the pasture behind him contentedly grazed on the lush grass. Overhead, birds snatched insects from the air and sang to each other. Lynn checked his bobber. *No nibbles, yet.*

School begins in a couple of weeks. I wonder if there will be new kids this year, and if classes will be difficult or easy? I hope none of my friends from across town have moved. I wonder if Sara will be in choir and band this year.

"Catch anything, Lynn?" asked Bob.

"No. I'm going home; I have no luck at all today."

Lynn eyes began to sting. Tears rolled down his cheeks. He felt bad that he wasn't chosenfor the ball game and hadn't caught any fish.

I had better not let Mom see me. She'll just get mad and criticize me for feeling bad.

Lynn approached his home from the back side so his mom couldn't see him and put his fishing gear in the shed. He took out a garden hoe, and began weeding the vegetable garden. Working carefully, Lynn removed weeds from the potatoes, squash, carrots, and green beans. Hearing a motor noise, he looked up and saw his dad coming with the rototiller.

Dad smiled at him. "Lynn, I am pleasantly surprised to find you out here weeding the garden. I am so proud of you. Did your mom tell you to do this?"

"No, she didn't. I wasn't chosen for a ball game and I didn't catch any fish. I got skunked by everyone else out there. Please don't tell Mom you found me here. She ordered me to go back to the ball game,

---

----

but I went fishing instead and after about an hour I came home and began weeding the garden."

"I won't tell Mom, but I am proud of you for weeding the garden. You are a good helper, Lynn. Thank you for what you did here."

"You're welcome, Dad. I enjoy helping you with the lawn and garden."

"Dad, supper is ready," called Lynn's mother. "Have you seen Lynn?"

"We're coming," shouted Lynn.

"Let's wash up, son. I'm hungry and I'll bet you are too."

"You got that right," answered Lynn. "Something smells really good."

"Lynn, did you play ball today?" asked his mom.

"No, Mom".

"What did you do then?"

"I went out and rode my bike," Lynn said.

"Where did you go?"

"I took my fishing pole and went to the river to fish-- caught nothing but insect bites. The trees, wild flowers, animals and other fishermen were nice—saw some friends who caught fish."

"Leave him alone, Honey, he's tired," his dad said.

"How can he be tired? He's done nothing."

"Hanging out is tiring," Lynn's dad said.

"I'm going to watch TV for a while," Lynn said.

"Okay, Son," his dad said. "I'll help Mom with the dishes."

Lynn searched the channels but couldn't find anything interesting, so he turned off the TV and picked up a book about the Civil War. At 9:30 PM he closed the book, yawned, said goodnight to his parents and went to bed.

"Dear God, bless my Mom and Dad. I'd like to be better at sports,

but don't have the ability. How can I improve if I can't play? Since I'm blind in one eye and have no depth perception, I can't gain the ability to judge the ball's approach to the plate, or where a fly ball will land. Show me what I should do. Please help Mom and me to get along better with each other. Thank you. Amen."

Forever Hopeful
Chapter Two

"Lynn, wake up," his mother said. She pulled the covers down to his feet. "It's time to eat your breakfast and get ready. We need to go to the mall and buy your school clothing."

"Mom, have some respect for my privacy. I'm tired. Yesterday I went fishing and weeded a big part of the garden before Dad came home from work. Let me sleep for a while."

"You'll get up and be ready to leave in 30 minutes. Thanks for doing the weeding, but I want to purchase your clothing for school today."

We always argue when we do this. I wish she would allow me to buy my own clothes.

But no, she has to have her say and chooses the worst looking clothing.

"Mom, why don't you give the money we'd spend on clothes to me? I will go by myself and you can do your thing at home?"

"I'm your mother and I will go with you to make sure you choose proper clothing."

"Oh, all right, I'm getting up. I'll be dressed and at the table in ten minutes."

"Be quicker. I'm making oatmeal."

Thirty minutes later, they arrived at the mall. Lynn's Mom took him into a men's clothing store and began searching the racks of khaki slacks. "Try this on to see if the size is right."

"Mom, that's clothes for old men, I'm fifteen. I want something like the rest of the fellows are wearing," Lynn said.

"You'll need some clothing for dress up occasions like dances and award's assemblies," his mother said.

"If I have to wear those clothes I won't go to dances."

"Of course you will. I'll call a nice young girl and arrange a date for you."

"Mom, you wouldn't do that, please, I'd be the laughing stock of the entire school. You know I don't like to dance."

"It's time you learned how to dance; maybe I'll sign you up for dance lessons."

"If I agree to two outfits from this store will you agree to two outfits from a store of my choice?" Lynn asked.

"Yes, as long as they are good outfits with no beer, tobacco advertising, or swear words."

"Mom, you know I do not smoke or drink alcohol. How about a shirt with a picture of a girl in a swimming suit?

"No, I should slap your face, Lynn."

"I was only teasing Mom, don't be upset."

"Try on these gray flannel slacks, Lynn. They will go nice with your cobalt blue shirt, your maroon shirt, and your green shirt."

"Mom, the only people at school who wear these clothes are the teachers and principal."

"Don't argue with me, Lynn, I'm your mother and know more about clothes than you."

Yeah, clothes worn only by old women and men who come to those tea parties you have at home. Dad won't even wear these styles of clothes, I can't say as I blame him.

"Mom, I'll be laughed out of school. Why waste your money? I will not wear these slacks or anything else you buy at this store to school."

"You will wear what I select to awards assemblies and dances, and you will like them."

"Fat chance that will happen," mumbled Lynn under his breath.

Lynn's mom chose shirts and pants and forced Lynn to try them on. Soon his mom was satisfied and made the purchases. Lynn and his mother left the store with his mom in tears.

"Now Mom, let's go to a store where they sell real clothes for boys or young men."

"Where is that?" asked Mom.

"The Brass Buckle. That's where all the kids from school go to buy their clothes."

Walking across the mall, Lynn's Mom saw other clothing stores and suggested clothing she saw in the window displays. Every suggestion by Lynn's mother brought the same response from Lynn, "No Mom, I don't like those clothes. They are not cool."

"But, Lynn, what will you wear during the winter? You'll need warmer clothing."

"That's not what I meant by cool clothes. I meant it's in style or what the other kids are wearing. I have sweaters and sweat shirts at home for the winter."

Maybe, After all, she is letting me choose some clothes from Brass Buckle. [overlapping printed line: *Lynn glanced at the tears in his mother's eyes.*]

"Mom, I haven't seen you smile yet today. You look like you are not happy. You seldom look up, but look toward the floor. There is no bounce in your walking, you just plod along with slumping shoulders and such a tight grip on your purse that your knuckles are white. You look like you could cry," Lynn said.

"Lynn, when we shop for your clothes we always argue. You don't like what I like. It seems like we fight over every article of clothing we buy. I just want you to look well dressed and you seem to like clothing that is not well made and fit only for working."

"Mom, you like to be in style and wear what other ladies wear. I want to wear the kinds of clothes like other kids at school are wearing. I won't buy clothes that are offensive to you or Dad, and certainly not something that is not proper. Kids like blue jeans and loose shirts. Dress up is for church. School clothes should be comfortable and cool."

"There's that word again. What does it mean?" asked his Mom.

"It means that it's what kids like, and feels good when we wear the clothes. It's in a kid's style," said Lynn. "Let's bring the clothes back that we bought at that other store."

"No, you need something for good and special occasions. You are a good student and win awards every year. The newspapers print pictures of the award winners and I don't want your picture in the

----

newspaper wearing clothing that is not proper. I insist you dress up for those occasions."

"For you, Mom, I will. Now will you smile, stand up straighter, and put a bounce in your step?

"Sure, son, I will."

When they arrived at The Brass Buckle, Lynn began looking through the many racks of clothes. Some showed tee shirts in a rainbow of colors; some with comments such as carpe diem, and others with advertised products. Lynn turned away from the advertisements. He chose one that had a picture of Curious George lying on his back, eyes closed, next to an open bottle of ether. He went back to the shirt with *carpe diem* on the front. "What does that mean?" his mother asked. "It certainly is not English."

"It means seize the day, make every minute count, do your best today."

"Well, that is a good motto for anyone. I approve of that shirt. I'm not sure of the Curious George shirt."

"That's just a fun shirt. You know how Curious George is into everything, always opening doors, boxes and bottles. This is one he should not have opened. It will cause a lot of laughs at school."

Lynn then walked over to the section of the store where the slacks and blue jeans were sold. Some of the jeans were faded, some had holes in them, some were dark blue, others light blue. There were gray jeans, blue jeans, green jeans, brown jeans, even white jeans. Lynn chose two, a pair of light blue denim jeans, and a brown pair of denim jeans.

At the checkout counter the cashier commented to Lynn's Mom, "Your son made some good choices."

"It's not what I would have chosen for him. I don't care for the clothing you sell here."

The clerk wisely said no more. Lynn whispered to the clerk, "You should see what she likes. I'll

look like an old man."

Lynn and his mother rode home in almost complete silence.

"Thank you for the clothes, Mom. I'll wear what you like to church and what I like to school."

Forever Hopeful

Chapter Three

"Lynn, come in the house; stop shooting that basketball." *Now what does she want? It seems like she's always after me for some reason. I wonder what I did wrong? I just can't seem to please her.*

"We need to go to the school building and register for your classes. Change your clothing to something better and then wash your face and hands and comb your hair."

"Is it necessary that I go, Mom? You did this without me when I was in grade school."

"I don't know what classes you want or need to take this year. We have not discussed those things."

Lynn sighed and put the basketball away, and walked toward his mother.

"I have to take Math, Science, English, Social Studies and physical education. I elect band, choir and study hall. Since band meets three days a week and choir the other two, that leaves physical education for three days and study hall two days. All this fills up the six periods for classes in a day." He closed the screen door behind him and turned on the kitchen faucet for a drink of water.

"That sounds like quite a heavy schedule, Lynn."

"Not too heavy. School is fun and I enjoy all of the classes. The more I can learn the better I will do in college. I do want to go to college and make something of myself."

"What would you study in college?"

Lynn's mother turned to the refrigerator and took out meat to thaw for supper.

"I don't know yet, Mom. There are so many choices. I should take an aptitude test to see where my interests and skills lie. The thing is I'm interested in all the courses I've studied so far. It will be difficult to choose."

"You go and clean up so we can go. After we are done at school we'll come home and eat lunch."

"What's for lunch, Mom?"

"Left over chicken, green beans, salad, rolls, with some left over apple pie."

"Sounds good." *Thank goodness it's not kraut and beans like we had yesterday. Yuk.*

Lynn went to his room and changed into his new blue jeans and carpe diem tee shirt. *I'd better change to black socks so Mom doesn't complain and make me change from my white socks. I will wear my newest gym shoes.*

"I'm ready to go, Mom."

"Let me look at you. Yes, you look nice."

While Mother drove to the school house, Lynn commented about his interest in gardening, music, and history.

"Could you make a living and support a family by studying those subjects?"

"Of course I could. If I study horticulture in college, I could teach at the college level—that is, if I earn a master's degree. If I study music I could teach anywhere from elementary school to college. If I study history I could teach high school or college level. There are many different areas of history. I could specialize in American history, European, World, Middle Ages, Ancient history. The list is almost endless."

"So, are you thinking of teaching school?"

"That's a possibility, Mom."

"Where would you teach?"

"I'd have to go to where ever there is a job available."

"I would hope you could find a job near home."

Soon they arrived at the school house and found a short line. The people seemed to move through the registration process at a reasonable rate of speed, since most students did not have much choice except for one elective. Lynn and his mother arrived at the table and were greeted by the school secretary and the high school principal.

"Hello, Lynn," both school officials said. "Did you have a good summer?"

"I suppose that depends on how you define 'good,'" said Lynn. "You know I'm blind in one eye, so I don't do well in sports, and since we live on the edge of town I see few of my classmates during the summer. I don't even get into trouble."

Everyone laughed at that comment about trouble.

"You of all people are least likely to have trouble or cause trouble. We

----

would have one wonderful school if everyone were like you, Lynn," both the secretary and principal said.

"Let's proceed with the registration process," the secretary said.

"You are required to study English which will be grammar and literature. You are a sophomore this year correct?"

"Yes, ma'am." Lynn leaned forward and put his elbows on the table.

"Social Studies will be World History from 3000 BCE to the present. Science will be Biology and Math will be geometry. I see you studied Algebra last year."

"Yes, ma'am.

"Now, about electives, what are your choices?" asked the principal.

"I want band again, and choir." Lynn smiled, looking at the principal.

"I'm required to take physical education, which alternates with study hall."

"All good choices," the principal said.

"I do have one question," Lynn said.

"And that is?" the principal asked.

"Well, Mom and I were talking about what I was going to do with my life and I am not sure yet, so my question is about an aptitude test to see where my skills and interests lie."

"That is a good question, Lynn. You will be given an aptitude test during English this fall and you should have the results before Thanksgiving Vacation."

The secretary said, "We need to pay for book rent which is $20 for each class, so that is a total of $80. We require a towel fee for gym class at $20 for the year. Lunch fees at $40 per month, and registration fee of $15. The total is $155."

"That is higher than last year by $30. It doesn't seem right that we have to pay all these fees. The taxes we pay should cover those costs. I don't know how some people pay these fees, we barely can and we have only one child. What do families with several children do?" Lynn's Mom said.

"The school board sets the fees; we just collect them," the principal said. "The school board meets tonight. You should go to the meeting and address your concerns to the board."

"I just might do that," mother said, standing up. They both shook the principal's hand and said goodbye.

After lunch, Lynn thought about the school year.   *I wonder if there will be any new students in school this fall.I hope Sara will be in choir and band again. She probably doesn't even know that I exist. Girls are different. I don't understand them. Sara is a pretty girl. She somehow seems different than other girls. I wish I could meet her and talk to her.*

Lynn passed the afternoon reading, shooting baskets and sorting his clothes. He hung the new slacks and shirts on hangers in his closet. Clothing that was too small for him he packed to be given away. Some clothing, too worn or ragged, he gave to his mother to be used for cleaning rags or thrown away.

When dinner was finished Lynn changed his clothes, picked up his Bible and said, "I'm going to church for the weekly youth group meeting." With his Bible in his book bag, Lynn rode his bicycle the six blocks to church. Upon arrival he noticed many of his classmates already there engaged in lively conversation.

He sat down in the back row, and watched others arrive.

To his surprise, Sara walked up to him and said, "Hello, Lynn; are you ready for school to start? I am."

"Hello, Sara. Yes, I'm ready. Summer vacation has become boring. Will you be in choir and band this year?"

"Yes, I will be. Will you be, too?"

"Yes, I am looking forward to both this year."

"Maybe we'll be in some other classes together, too."

"That would be fun, Sara."

As Sara walked forward in the church to talk with other girls, Lynn pumped his fist in the air and said a silent "Yes!" *I guess I was wrong, she does know I exist.*

The pastor called the meeting to order, opened with prayer, and the group sang a bouncy, happy little tune about Noah's ark that soon had the group smiling and laughing over the lyrics.

He told a joke about a preacher who bought a horse that would start walking when the rider said, "Praise the Lord," and stop when the rider said, "Amen." While riding, the horse became frightened by a snake and began to gallop away. The preacher held on tightly and shouted "Stop, stop, whoa." The horse continued to run toward a tall cliff while the preacher frantically kept shouting "stop" and "whoa." Finally he remembered to say "Amen" six times which brought the horse to a stop three feet from the edge of the cliff. The rider with shaking hands removed his handkerchief from his pocket, mopped his brow and loudly said, "Praise the Lord."

Everyone in the group laughed or smiled; soon they had tears in their eyes from their laughter. When they calmed down the pastor said, "It is time for tonight's lesson. It is called the Roman Road. If you have your Bible along, turn to the New Testament and find the book of Romans, right after Acts."

When everyone was ready; he began by saying, "When we love someone we want the best of everything for that person. The Bible is God's love story to human kind. God wants what is best for us. He wants to be in a close personal relationship with every person on earth. People from earliest times wandered away from God. God worked out a way for people to have a personal relationship with Himself.

"He sent His Son, Jesus, to take on human flesh and live among people for thirty-three years. He was born to Mary and Joseph and grew up just like any other child. When Jesus was thirty years old, He began His ministry that lasted three years. He preached and healed people, and did many other miracles.

"Then He died on a Roman cross. Jesus was human like us, but He was sinless. He satisfied God's plan by dying on the cross—thus taking the punishment for our sins. The third day, he rose from the dead victorious over sin, death, and the devil. Jesus was the sinless sacrifice to take away our sins and make us right with God. To claim God's plan for ourselves, we need to confess our sins and ask Jesus to live in our lives. How do we do that you may ask? Follow me down the Roman Road and you'll find the way. We're using the NIV this time.

"First, Romans 3:23. Lynn will you read that verse out loud. Thank you."

Lynn read, "For all have sinned and fall short of the glory of God."

"That verse tells us we all are sinners and cannot meet God's requirement of sinlessness. Sara will you find and read Romans 6:23?"

Sara read, "For the wages of sin is death but the gift of God is eternal life through Jesus Christ our Lord."

"This verse tells us that God provided a way for us to be right with Him. That gift was and is Jesus Christ our Lord."

"Mary, will you find and read Romans 5:8 please?"

Mary read, "But God commended His love toward us, in this: while we were still sinners, Christ, died for us."

"That means that Jesus died on purpose to pay for our sins. He didn't have to, but He did it out of love for us."

"Sam, will you find Romans 10:13?"

Sam read, "For everyone who calls on the name of the Lord will be saved."

"This verse means that if you call on God to save you, you will be saved. It is the best guarantee ever written."

"Susan, please find Romans 10:9."

Susan read, "That if you confess with your mouth Jesus is Lord and believe in your heart that God raised Him from the dead, you will be saved."

"Now, I want you to quietly think about what we just read and I explained to you. When you have thought about those verses you may quietly leave your seat. If you want to talk to me about accepting Jesus as your Savior tonight I will be in my office, and will talk with any of you."

With those words said, the pastor left the room and the youth group. Lynn watched him go. *It sure seems like he was talking directly to me. I felt something. I don't know what is telling me to go talk to the pastor.* Lynn rose from his chair and quietly walked to the pastor's

----

office and knocked on the door. When the pastor opened the door he smiled at Lynn and invited him to take a seat. Closing the door he sat behind his desk and asked, "How may I help you?"

"I felt the urge to talk to you during our trip down the Roman Road. I want to accept Jesus as my Savior."

"Oh, Lynn, praise God. You know that all you need to do is confess your sins, believe that God raised Jesus from the dead, and ask Jesus to live in and control your life. If you do that you'll be saved and spend eternity with God. Do you want to pray that prayer now?"

"Yes, I do."

"Okay, begin when you are ready."

"I'm ready now." He closed his eyes and folded his hands.

"Jesus, I know I am a sinner in need of your salvation. Please forgive my sins. I believe God raised you from the dead and I want you to live in my life and take control of my life. In your name I pray. Amen."

"Welcome to the family of God, Lynn."

Lynn felt a peace and joy he had never known. When he arose to leave, another knock sounded on the door. As the pastor opened the door for Lynn to leave, he saw another person from the youth group waiting.

"Come in and have a seat."

"Good bye, Lynn, see you in church Sunday."

Lynn left the church feeling happy. He looked forward to school and home-work. In the parking lot, he saw Sara talking to Rachael, one of their classmates. When he drew near to them, they stopped their talking and Sara smiled. "Well, Lynn, school starts next week;

---

enjoy the rest of the summer vacation. I'll see you in band and choir, and maybe in other classes as well."

"I hope so. You enjoy the rest of your summer, Sara, and you too, Rachael. See you in school next week.

Forever Hopeful

Chapter Four

The week before classes began passed quickly. Lynn practiced his trombone more than usual. His mom came into his bedroom while he was practicing: "Lynn, must you play so loud? I have a guest downstairs for tea; I can barely hear her speak."

"Mom, I'm not playing that loud."

"Take that instrument outside and play behind the garage."

"How can I improve if I do not practice?"

"You can improve behind the garage."

Lynn obediently gathered his instrument, music and music stand and took them behind the garage. As he practiced he noticed that he was hearing birds singing with his playing. When he stopped for a little while, the birds stopped singing. When he started again, the birds began singing again.

Tony rode his bicycle around the corner of the garage and sneered. "So this is where all the racket is coming from. I'm going to call the cops, you're disturbing the peace."

"Be quiet, Tony. The birds are singing along with my playing, and no one else has complained."

"Maybe all your neighbors are deaf and can't hear all this racket."

"Goodbye, Tony."

"Goodbye, dummy, expect a visit from the cops."

The first day of school arrived with Lynn eager to begin classes.

After packing his backpack with books, paper, pens and pencils, Lynn was ready for all of his classes. Since band would not meet the first day, he left his instrument at home. When he arrived at the school building he saw several groups of students congregated on the walks and lawns in front of the building.

The bike rack was nearly full. Long yellow school buses

disgorged both laughing and serious students. Lynn could see who was new to the school and who was a returning student. The new students were quiet and the returning students called out to their friends. Some students arrived and stepped out of parent's cars while many older students, the seniors in particular, arrived in cars, pickup trucks, scooters and mopeds.

What a noisy place! Cars with loud mufflers, one with no muffler, a few with glass pack mufflers. The bell rang irritatingly loud. Some students smiled at the thought of a new school year beginning, a few moaned, but most just walked into the school building in quiet conversation with their friends. Being a sophomore, Lynn knew his locker would be on the third floor so he climbed the staircase shoulder to shoulder with many other students. He found his locker and was disappointed that it didn't open the first or second time he tried the combination lock. A teacher walked up and offered to help. Soon the locker was open, and the teacher explained how the combination worked properly. Tony saw the entire episode and, with sarcasm in his voice, said, "For someone who thinks he is so smart, how come you can't work a simple combination lock?" Lynn didn't say anything in return, but turned and walked down the hall to his first class which was English. The tardy bell hadn't rung yet so Lynn watched groups of students talking in the hall. The boys were loud and slapping each other on the shoulder or back, wishing each other well.

The girls stood and talked in quiet whispers as they watched the boys. Sometimes they laughed quietly while they watched certain boys. *Why are the boys so loud and girl so quiet, always whispering and laughing as they watch the boys? The girls are pretty, but hard to figure out.* Soon the bell rang for class to start and to Lynn's surprise Sara was seated to his left across the aisle. Sara looked at him, smiled and said, "Hello Lynn."

Lynn felt his face grow warm, but he managed to say, "Good morning, Sara."

Just then the fire alarm rang. "What do we do now?" a new student asked.

"Follow me to the nearest exit," Lynn said, and then out to the curb. "This is early for a fire drill so it has to be a prank."

"Who would do that?" a girl asked.

"I think I know who, and I'm sure the principal has him cornered already." Sure enough, the principal was leading Tony to his office. Soon Tony came out side with a frown on his face.

"Hey, Tony, several students yelled, what did you get for punishment?"

"Why pick on me?"

"Any time a prank happens we know you are probably behind it."

"I guess I'll have to change my pranks."

"What did the principal do to you?"

"Nothing much, just read the riot act to me and gave me a detention. Then he said when I have five of them I'm out of school for a week."

"You'd better be careful, Tony."

At that moment, the bell to return to class rang.

The day passed quickly and to Lynn's surprise, Sara was also in his Social Studies class. Choir was the last class of the day and they did a lot of warm up singing along with a couple of songs from the previous year. The director announced the choir had been asked to sing two songs at the annual Veterans Day ceremonies in November." One of the songs will be "Over There" and the other will be "The Last Time I Saw Paris." We will wear good school clothing. I will not expect you to dress in your Sunday best." At that announcement a big sigh of relief issued from the members of the choir. "Would you rather dress up?" asked the director.

"No, definitely not," answered the choir.

The director smiled and said, "That was just to see if you were listening."

The bell rang and Lynn walked to his locker. He had to read the first chapter in the Social Studies text book about the Sumerians from 3000 B. C. so he tucked the book in his back pack.

"Hey, dud, did you do anything worthwhile today?" asked Tony.

"I sure did, Tony. My classes are great, the teachers are great, and this will be an excellent year."

"You are going to sit at home every night with your nose in a book? Why don't you get a life and play football? Oh, that's right you're a loser, you'd fumble the ball or run to the wrong goal line."

"Goodbye, Tony. I need to go to the library to start doing my homework."

"That stuffy old place. Go to some place interesting like Hardee's."

"Too noisy. I can't concentrate there."

"What does concentrate mean?"

"Look it up in the dictionary, Tony, you'll learn something. Rachael, help Tony look up concentrate."

"No time now, we're going for a coke and fries at Hardee's."

Tony and Rachael laughed as they walked away. Other girls and boys only scratched their heads, whispered to each other and laughed.

Lynn closed his locker, walked down the stairs and through the hall toward the school door. A few girls and boys called his name and said, "Hello," and then the girls whispered and looked away.

Girls are hard to figure out, they giggle a lot and whisper a lot. I wonder if anyone except them knows why they do that. Do they whisper good things about people or bad things? Do they spread rumors? I'm glad Sara is in English and Social Studies with me as well as band and choir. Maybe she can help me understand.

The weekend came and Lynn argued with his Mom again.

"Mom, I really don't have time to go to the Youth Group meeting tonight."

"You will go and spend some time with people near your age."

"Mom, I have school work to do."

"Don't argue with me, I'm your Mother and I say you will go. There is an old saying that all work and no play make Jack a dull boy."

"I'll go next week, Mom."

"Lynn, I agree with your Mother," said his dad. We appreciate that you want to earn good grades and we are proud of you and what you've accomplished. But at Youth group, you'll learn more about

---

God and Jesus, have a good time with the other kids and get to know them better."

"Oh, all right, I'll go tonight."

That night Lynn walked to church for the meeting, wishing he could have stayed at home to do homework. The Bible lesson was about Gideon and how God used him to defeat some of Israel's enemies with just 300 men. The pastor explained that when Gideon called for men to fight the enemy 32,000 came to fight. "Too many men," God said. All who were afraid were allowed to go home. At that time 22,000 men went home. Only 10,000 remained. "Still too many men," God said. Another test left only 300 men to fight against the enemy.

"Dear God, we'll all die in this battle with only 300 men," Gideon prayed.

"You'll win, just trust me," God said. "Now, Gideon; supply each man with a clay pitcher, a torch, and be sure they each have their sword along. At the time for the battle position the men around the enemy camp. They are to set the torch on fire, place it inside the pitcher, and at your signal they will break the pitcher, hold the torch high and shout as loud as possible, "The sword of the Lord and Gideon!" I'll take care of the rest of the fight."

"Some of the men shook their heads and said, "Maybe I should have gone home earlier. This is the strangest battle plan ever dreamed up."

"After the sun set and everything was dark, the men quietly stationed themselves around the camp of the enemy, lit their torches and held them inside their pitchers.

"I sure hope this works," whispered several soldiers.

Soon a light appeared and Gideon shouted, "The sword of the Lord and Gideon." The sound echoed down the valley and bounced off the hills. The enemy ran out of their tents and began wildly swinging their swords at anyone. They were killing their own soldiers and others were running away from the carnage. When daylight broke in the East, the soldiers of Israel saw the results of the fight. Not one Israelite soldier had died, but thousands of the enemy lay still on the ground. The Israelites picked up every valuable item they could find.

The pastor summed up the lesson by saying that "a great victory had been won because Gideon had answered God's call to him and he trusted God for the victory."

"Later it was learned from some captured enemy soldiers that when the pitchers were broken and the Israelites shouted, the enemy thought they were severely outnumbered and in their confusion and attempts to escape they had destroyed each other."

"What did you learn from this Bible lesson?" asked the pastor.

"Trust in God and yield to Him and you'll always be successful," answered Sara.

"That is an excellent answer, Sara. With God's help you can do anything successfully."

"Now," He looked around at the group. "I have a plan that I need some help with, and I'd like Sara to be the committee chair person to plan a picnic for two weeks from tonight."

Cheers rose from the youth group. Comments of, "Oh good," were heard.

"Quiet please," the pastor said. "Sara, you have a request or comment?"

"I'll be glad to do the job. I'll need some help from both boys and girls. If I call you, please say "yes, I'll help."

Sara immediately began to make a list of names trying to include an equal number of boys and girl. The pastor dismissed the meeting. Lynn rose to leave the church, but was stopped by Sara's hand on his arm.

"Lynn, I'd like for you to help on the food committee. Ask about two boys and two girls to help you. Sit down and choose four names from my list while I go and ask Tony to be in charge of some simple games."

"This sounds like fun, Sara. I'm glad you asked me to help."

"I knew I could count on you, Lynn. Try to meet with your group before Wednesday and write down what foods you decide on and let's meet at the library after school on Friday."

Sara approached Tony. Tony squirmed on his chair and looked pleadingly at Sara. "Please, not me, ask someone else." After a little persuasion by Sara, Tony agreed to the same schedule.

At the Friday meeting, Tony scowled and placed his elbows on the table. "I don't like this," he mumbled. "Sara," said Tony, "don't ask me to help again. I've never done this before and I had to ask my mother for help. I was never so embarrassed in my life."

Sara was careful not to laugh.

"I've been teased and called Mama's boy for the entire week."

"I'm sorry, Tony, but looking at your list of games I'd say you did very well with your group and your Mom's help." Sara smiled and said, "Thanks Tony,"

Sliding his chair back, Tony said, "Don't tell anyone my Mom helped me."

"What about Dud over there, how did he do? Did he drop the ball again?"

"Tony, we'll have no name calling here," Sara said.

"Lynn, do you have the food list?"

"Yes. We chose to have healthy foods such as carrot sticks, celery sticks, burgers with buns and all the condiments. For drinks we will use bottled water.

Tony just groaned, while covering his eyes.

Sara smiled and said, "Good work by your groups. The games sound like fun, and the food sounds wonderful. I am anxious for next Sunday evening.

Forever Hopeful

Chapter Five

The week between the committee meeting and the picnic passed quickly. Lynn felt nervous about going; there would be lots of people there. When he arrived he sat on a lawn chair off to the side of the group. Lynn saw Tony sit down and elbow his friend Bob. "Let's go and give Lynn a bad time," Tony said.

"Okay, Tony, let's tease him about his lack of ability in every sport."

"Hey loser," called Tony when he and Bob approached Lynn.

"Will you join any of the games tonight? If he does, Bob, don't choose him for your team, he loses every game he plays."

Lynn didn't say anything; he just sat on his chair and considered the source of the comment.

Why is he so negative all the time? It's beyond my ability to understand. He could do better in his classes if he didn't have sports on his mind all the time. Or maybe he feels inferior because of his grades. He has no friends; no one wants to be around someone who is constantly making cruel remarks about others. I hope Tony changes his attitude. Soon Tony and Bob left Lynn when he did not become angry and return Tony's insults.

Rachael stopped and asked Lynn why there weren't any soft drinks or cake or ice cream to eat at the picnic.

"Rachael, the foods we chose are better for your health and well-being than all those sugary foods."

"That may be, Lynn, but they are not much fun to eat."

"Rachael, you are a good kid, but are you happy when you look in a mirror? In health class we learned that those foods you mentioned can cause skin problems such as pimples and almost uncontrollable weight gain."

"I know, but I enjoy them so much better than all those carrot and celery sticks."

At that moment the pastor and his wife approached Lynn and Rachael. "Hello Lynn, Rachael," the pastor's wife said. "Rachael, I overheard what Lynn said about sugary foods. He is right you know. I wouldn't say this if I didn't care about you. If you eliminated the soft drinks, you'll lose some weight.

"I disagree," said Rachael. "I don't think they're all that bad. If they are, why hasn't the Food and Drug Administration removed them from the market. Look at Tony, he doesn't have a weight problem and his face is clear."

"That's because he is so active in all the sports he participates in and he runs all those calories off. Do you exercise, Rachael?" asked the pastor's wife.

"No, I don't. It makes me tired. I'd rather watch TV."

Tony called out, "The games will begin in five minutes. There will be a three-legged sack race, and a free-throw shooting contest with a basketball for the winner. Also a marble contest, paint your friends arm, restyle your girlfriend's or boyfriend's hair with the winners' pictures in the next church newsletter. The winner of the bubble-blowing contest with bubblegum will receive a free checkup

----

---

at Dr. Jin's Dental Clinic. For the contest among the girls to see who has the longest hair, the winner gets a free hair cut at the Mane Salon.

Pastor has the scale for the boy's weight contest and the pastor's wife has the tape measure for the girl's hair. Our beloved sponsor has the bubble gum and I, Tony, have the basketball for the free throw contest. Rachael has the burlap sacks for the three legged race. Lynn has the marbles and paint. Sara has the combs and hair spray to reset your friend's hair. Everyone must participate in at least two games. Ready, set, go, and best wishes."

Everyone scrambled toward the location for their choice of a game. Soon lots of laughter could be heard with screams as the girls looked in the mirrors after the boys had restyled their hair.

When the girls' hair had been measured, the girls all quickly conceded that Angie had the longest hair. Even in a ponytail she could sit on it. Angie had glowing black hair that she admitted she curls with a curling iron at the end of the pony tail.

"Angie, you hair is so beautiful, how do you keep it so nice?" asked Barbie.

"I wash it every day before I go to school."

Nina, the youth sponsor's wife, ran the camera.

"Hey, Tony, which game are you going to play?" Lynn asked.

"I'm going to show all these amateurs how to sink free-throws."

"Hey, everyone," Lynn called, "Tony thinks he can show us how to sink free-throws. When everyone had gathered, Lynn called, "any time you are ready, hot shot." Everyone laughed.

"Tony," Lynn reminded him, "the contest is 24 shots. The one with the most free throws made is the winner."

Tony went to the line and dribbled the ball a few times. Closing one eye he lofted the ball toward the basket. Swish! It didn't strike the iron, but went right through. Lynn threw the ball back to him.

"That's one," everyone called.

A couple more dribbles and another shot went through the hoop. All the boys cheered. The same thing happened with shots three through ten.

"I've got to have a drink of water," Tony said.

"Here you are, hot shot," Mary Ann said.

Tony walked back to the line and dribbled the ball a few more times.

"Why does he always bounce the ball a few times before he shoots?" Sara asked.

"That helps him concentrate and relax a bit," Lynn said.

Two more dribbles and up the ball flew, bounced off the backboard and dropped through the hoop. "That makes eleven out of eleven shots," Lynn said.

Again Tony shot the ball and watched it drop through the hoop. "Twelve," Tony said.

"You're half way there," said Joe.

Tony picked up the ball and quickly shot eight more times. Each time the ball went through the hoop. "I've got to have another drink. How many have I made now?"

"You've made twenty out of twenty with no misses," all the girls shouted.

"Can I quit now?" Tony asked.

"No, you still have four more shots," Joe said.

Tony took out his handkerchief and wiped his forehead and hands. "Okay, give me that pumpkin," Everyone laughed at the comment.

Tony again dribbled the ball and shot it towards the backboard. Instead it hit the back of the rim and bounced into the air and then fell through the hoop. On the next shot the ball hit the top of the front of the rim, bounced off the backboard and fell through the hoop.

"That's twenty two out of twenty two. Tony, you're hot today," Rachael said.

Grasping the ball, Tony dribbled five times, bent his knees, and with one eye closed lofted the ball toward the basket.

"Tony, a perfect shot," Lynn said. "I say a good show ole chap. One more time, Tony."

Everyone held their breath as Tony toed the free throw line. Tony again wiped the sweat from his forehead and rubbed his hands on his blue jeans. He grasped the ball and dribbled it five more times, bent his knees, raised the ball over his head and shot it through the air. Everyone held their breath as the ball struck the top edge of the front of the rim, bounced against the middle of the back board, dropped back against the top of the front edge of the rim, and slowly rolled into the hoop.

The crowd jumped up and down and ran to slap Tony on the back, cheering and shouting congratulations. "You did it, Tony!" they shouted. "Way to go hot shot."

Tony just smiled. "I knew I could do it," he said.

Rachael won the bubble gum contest and immediately declined the dental checkup. Steve restyled his girlfriend's hair by placing it all on top of her head and held it there with hair pins and hair spray. Barbie restyled Steve's hair by combing it all straight back which

---

made it hang below his shoulders. Tom was the winner of the painted arm contest. The heaviest boy volunteered to eat all the remaining food after everyone had their fill.

Soon all the teasing began. "Steve, I can tell you've not studied hair styling. Barbie's hair looks like a blond hay stack. If you baled it you might get 20 bales." Barbie just laughed.

"Leave your hair the way Barbie styled it, Steve. You look better."

"Lynn painted a large green snake on my arm so I can scare my Mom," said Tim.

With the winners all declared and the laughter diminishing, Pastor folded his hands, closed his eyes, and prayed, "Father, thank you for these young people here and the fun we had with these games. We ask for your blessing on the food and fellowship, in Jesus name, Amen

Lynn helped with the serving along with Sara, then he took his plate of food and went to sit alone at the edge of the group. Soon Sara came by Lynn and asked if she could sit by him.

"I -I -I would like that Sara." Nervously, Lynn shifted in his chair.

"Lynn, are you enjoying your classes?"

"Y—yes, Sara, I like school as you know. I especially like the World History class and English."

"How about your classes, Sara. Which do you like best?" "I like band and choir, but I really enjoy English, as you do, and also science. I must admit that Math is not easy for me. I really have to work hard on that subject to receive a good grade."

"I find Math easy. I usually go to the public library after school because it is quiet there and I concentrate better. Would you come to the library, too, and we could help each other with our school assignments?"

"Do they allow that?"

"If a few people whisper no one will complain" replied Lynn.

"Do you go there every night? I need to be home by six to help my Mom with dinner, so with school dismissed at 3:30 that gives me about two hours of study time."

"I'll be there tomorrow night," said Lynn. "What do you want to do when you finish school, Sara?"

"I think teaching, nursing, or science research. What about you, Lynn? What do you want to do with your life?"

"I'm not sure; maybe teach history, or become a math teacher—who knows, I might even become a Pastor. I'd like to help kids find their place in life," said Lynn.

"I'd like to help people who are ill to become well again," said Sara. "I do not like all the diseases that plague the world, along with hunger and fighting."

"Me too, Sara. I think you have some good goals."

"You do as well, Lynn."

"It looks like the party is breaking up and I see your father is here to take you home. I'll see you on Monday at school."

Lynn walked home from the party with many thoughts filling his mind. *Sara impresses me. She is sincere, kind, studious, and a wonderful person. I hope we can be friends. If I treat her with kindness and respect maybe we can develop a friendship. I certainly hope so, being alone all the time is quite lonely. I'd like a friend like Sara.*

Forever Hopeful

Chapter Six

"Lynn, what are you doing in your bedroom all the time? Every day you go to school and after dinner you go to your room and your dad and I don't see you until the next morning."

"Now, honey, he is doing his school work. He has quite a class load. He's trying to do good work. We had a good talk at dinner tonight about his classes and about the young people's picnic last week. That picnic sounded like a lot of fun."

"But I want to see more of him. I'm his mother and I want to spend time with him," she whined.

"Mom, earning good grades is important to me. Dad is right that I have a heavy class load, but the class load is manageable. I'm happy that you care about me. If I can earn good grades maybe I can earn a scholarship or two to pay part of my college expenses."

"I'm all for that," Dad said.

"I wish I could see you more often than just breakfast and dinner," said Mom.

"Honey, stop complaining. Let Lynn do his homework. He goes to church with us on Sunday so we have that time with him. I'm proud of my son and I feel we need to let him study."

"I feel I'm being cheated out of time that, as his mother, I'm entitled to."

As they left Lynn's room he returned to his studies. A thought crept into his mind. *I would like to spend more time with her, too. But I think she complains too much and seems to want only her way in things.*

Lynn continued to study each night and go to classes each day.

The last Friday of September the Social Studies teacher greeted the class with a smile and then announced an assignment to be due on the last Friday of October.

"Your assignment will be to choose an ancient civilization such as Sumer, Greece, or Rome and report on general aspects of that civilization. You'll need information about the government, industries, agriculture, and where it is located on a map. Note whether they were a war-like people or a peaceful society. I expect your assignment to be a minimum of 1000 words, and more if you can find the resources. You must have an outline of your paper, and at least four sources that are not from an encyclopedia. Are there any questions?"

Tony asked, "What do you mean by sources that are not in an encyclopedia"

"Good question, Tony. The encyclopedia is generally the first place students your age go to, but that is good only for general information, not specific information. The library here at school has other Social Studies text books, and if you know someone who teaches history, ask to interview them. The National Geographic publishes articles on historical topics as well as geography and most high school and college libraries keep back issues. Maybe someone you know has traveled to an area of interest to you and came home with information about that nation's history. Ask for an interview. Colleges especially have a site on their computers called The Reader's Guide to Periodical Literature. These books list topics in alphabetical order and tell which magazine you will find the topic in along with

---

the year it was published and the page number on which the article begins. So there you have text books, persons to interview, magazines, and the Reader's Guide."

"Yes, Maggie, what is your question?"

"Must we type our report? Does it need a title page? What about a bibliography?"

"Good questions, Maggie. You must have done reports like this before. Yes, you should have all three of those things in your report. All of you have access to a computer, if not at home, the school has several you may use."

"Imagine a blank sheet of paper. About 1/3 of the page down from the top, center your title in all capital letters. Divide the paper in half from side to side and center your full name, no nick names please. About 1/3 of the way up from the bottom, center my name as your instructor and the calendar date the report is due. Remember the last Friday in October. Now here is a little advice to make this easier. Spend some time at the library on Saturday to see how much information is available on your topic. Every year, I have one or two students panic the last week before the report is due saying they cannot find information on their topic. Do yourself a favor; find out how much is information is available on, let's say, the Edomites or Amalekites. Look before you choose a topic."

During breakfast the next day, Lynn announced: "I need to go to the Public Library to begin research on a Social Studies project."

His mother choked on her pancake. "More homework?"

"Yes, it's about an ancient civilization of my choosing."

"I thought you would be home today, since it is a Saturday. I seldom get to see you once school starts. I think I'll talk to the principal about your homework."

Lynn gazed at her. *Is she serious or just complaining?*

"You may talk to him, Mom, but it will do no good. He will not change the assignment. It is part of the learning process."

"I'm going to give him a piece of my mind. The school makes the students study too much."

"Mom, stay at home. You'll just embarrass yourself and me."

"Honey, Lynn is correct. The principal will not change the way a teacher teaches unless it is illegal or immoral. Lynn needs to learn these things before college. Colleges expect their students to know how to do research. If you insist on going to the principal with this complaint, I'll not go with you."

"I thought you were my husband and supported me," she said angrily crossing her arms and stomping her foot.

"I am, but I will not support you in this matter. I love you, but I cannot support this notion of yours."

Lynn left the house thinking, *I'm glad Dad said what he did, Mom seems to want to dominate everyone and everything she comes in contact with.*

When Lynn arrived at the library he found Sara already there surrounded by books. When she looked up and recognized Lynn she smiled and said, "Hi, Lynn. I'll bet you are here for the same reason I am; our research project for Social Studies. Have you chosen a topic?"

"Not yet, I'm leaning toward Greece, the ancient city state of Athens."

"I was thinking of Rome".

"Why don't we help each other to see how much information is available?"

"Good idea, two heads are better than one, especially in this situation. What have you found on Rome so far?" Lynn asked.

"Nothing yet, I just pulled these books off the shelves. The librarian watched me and the more I pulled out, the more she frowned," giggled Sara. "Sit by me, Lynn, and let's see what we can find on the Greek city state of Athens. The librarian will probably question us as to our motives."

"I'd like to sit by you, It will save us a great deal of time."

"I agree. Look here is a book on ancient Greece."

"I found two on Greek city states."

"Good for you, Lynn. I didn't know research could be so much fun."

"A task is always fun and easier when a friend works with another friend," Lynn said.

"I'd like to be friends."

"So would I."

Soon Lynn and Sara had added several more books to the table. Just then the librarian stopped at the table. "You two certainly have a lot of books here. What are you doing?"

"We were assigned a research project on an ancient civilization of our choosing. We are looking to see how much information is available on ancient Rome and the Greek city state of Athens."

"Do you mind if I help you?" asked the librarian.

"Of course not," Sara said.

    "May I show you the Reader's Guide on the computer here at the library?   Did your instructor discuss this with you?" asked the librarian.

"Yes, he did, but we had not gotten that far yet," said Sara.

"Follow me to our computer laboratory." When they were seated there, the librarian showed them how to access the Reader's Guide to Periodical Literature. "After you have booted your computer, type into the search engine, Reader's Guide to Periodical Literature, place the cursor over the search box and press the enter key. Soon you will see this screen appear. Notice there is another search box at the top."

"So, Sara, what is your topic?"

"My topic is the Roman Empire."

"When I type Roman Empire, notice near the top of the page, under where you typed your topic, the blue bar that says, results 1-10 of about 57,753. You see a title, and maybe a picture of a book cover. Under that the author's name then it lists, Book, so you know this is a book, not a written magazine article. Next to that it says Juvenile Audience. Now you know that this book was written for someone about your age. Next it lists the language the book uses for the text, and last of all the publisher, in this case World Book/Two Can of Chicago, Illinois published in 1996.

"As you scroll down the page you'll see a list of 10 book titles. Next to the bottom of the page you will see another blue bar and at the right hand side you find, First Prev 1, 2, 3. If you click on 2, low and behold another list of books on the Roman Empire. We'll stop here. I'm sure you know what will be on page 3 and so on. Finally at item 72 we find something that is not a book. This one says it is a film strip. Item 73 is an e-book.

"Next I'll type into the search box, 'Periodical Magazines about the Roman Empire, then place my cursor over 'about the Roman Empire.' Now I need to pick and choose the magazine I want."

"Let's click on a title and see what happens. I now see a brief summary of what the book or article is about. If I scroll down, I see a list of libraries where I can find the actual book."

The librarian straightened up and smiled at them. "Now you know how to use the computer to find more sources of information about your topic."

"We also have several magazines that may be of help to you in researching your topics. If you'll follow me again, I'll show you where we keep back issues of those magazines we subscribe to." The librarian led them up a flight of stairs and turned on a light to reveal a large room filled with stacks of magazines.

"This takes up a lot of space, surely there is an easier, less space consuming way to store all this information," said Lynn.

"There is, we used to do it on microfilm, but now we put the magazines on compact disks. We could take this entire room and store the information here on three shelves of compact disks. Let's find your magazines."

Soon with compact disks in hand Sara and Lynn returned to the table. They began to divide the books into piles of Rome and Greece. Taking out notebooks and pens they began to read and take notes on the information. Working steadily, Lynn and Sara worked their way through most of the books when Sara noticed the time.

"Lynn, it is after 12:30. I'm hungry and need to go home."

"I guess I'm hungry too. May I plan to meet you here again Monday after school?"

"I would like that. We could continue to study and complete homework assignments here at the library."

"Since we live only a couple of blocks from each other may I walk to your house with you?"

"Sure, I'd like that."Lynn and Sara walked home each carrying several books for their assignment. "Sara, what do you think of this assignment?"

"I think it is excellent. We will have to do so much of this kind of homework in college and this is a good way to learn how to do research. I find researching a topic is interesting and even exciting. I think that by the time I have written the paper I'll have more than the 1000 word limit. The more I have in information, the more I will have learned.

"I hope we have to do more of this kind of assignment. I'm going to save the papers and keep them for when I am in college. I figure they will give me a good start on college papers."

"Good idea, Lynn, I think I'll do the same. I want to thank you for helping me today. I don't think the librarian would have come and helped us if I was there alone."

"Thank you for helping me. You are a good friend. Here we are in front of your home. I'll say good bye and see you in church tomorrow and at school on Monday. I'll also see you at the library after school. Have a good day."

"You too, Lynn.

Forever Hopeful

Chapter Seven

"Lynn, there's a telephone call for you. A young lady named Sara wants to speak with you," called his Dad from the foot of the stairs.

"I'll be right down." Lynn hurried down the stairs two steps at a time. Picking up the phone he said, "Hello, Sara."

"Hi, Lynn. Joe and Nina, the youth group sponsors from church, called and asked me to come to their house to help plan the party. They asked that I call you and ask you to come and help with the planning."

"I'll be at your house in about 10 minutes, Sara."

"Dad and Mom, Sara and I have been asked by Joe and Nina to help plan a party for the youth group from church. Sara and I will ride our bikes to Joe and Nina's house to plan the party."

"Who is Sara?" asked Lynn's Mom.

"Sara is a friend from church and school. You've seen her. She has dark hair that she keeps short and wavy. She has brown eyes and stands about 5' 8" tall. She is in the school choir same as me along with band and two of my classes."

"You've had your eyes open haven't you son," teased his Dad.

"Yes, we've seen her at church and, from what we've seen and heard, she is a nice girl."

"Aw, Dad, she is just a friend. Not a girlfriend, only a friend."

"I understand, son, I was only teasing you. I'm glad you have friends."

"Thanks, Dad, I'll be at Joe and Nina's home. I don't know when we will be finished, but I'll be home when we are through."

Riding to Sara's house, Lynn wondered what kind of party they would help plan. He knocked on the door. Sara's Dad soon opened it. "Hello, Lynn, come into the house," said Mr. Brown. "Sara will be here in just a minute; she's changing her shoes."

"Thanks, Mr. Brown." He saw Sara coming down the hall.

"Hello, Lynn," said Sara with a smile on her face and in her voice. "Shall we go to Joe and Nina's house now?"

"Sure, the sooner we start, the sooner we will be finished."

Soon they arrived at the sponsors' home. Joe met them at the front door and asked them to walk around to the back of the house to the deck. There sat Nina with books on party planning.

"Hello, Sara and Lynn, Thanks for coming to help plan the Halloween party."

"We are planning a Halloween party? That sounds like fun," said Sara and Lynn in unison.

Joe joined them and quickly asked them what Nina had told them.

"Just that the party would have a Halloween theme," said Sara. Soon Bob and Sally joined them and the planning began in earnest. Passing out books with sections on Halloween parties, the teenagers soon found party suggestions. Sally found a game about ducking for apples. Bob found a game about pinning the hat on the scarecrow. "Boo," said Lynn, "that sounds too elementary."

"Are you afraid you'll miss the scarecrow?" teased Sara.

"No, I'd probably miss the whole board." Everyone laughed.

I'm afraid I'll miss everything and Sara will think I'm dumb and not want to be my friend anymore.

Joe announced that he thought a hay ride would be fun. "Of course," the teens cheered. "Okay, the first item is a hay ride," said Nina as she wrote on her list. "Do any of you men know of a farmer with a tractor or a team of horses to pull the hay wagon?"

"Yes," said Bob.

"Call him right now," said Joe.

Bob reached into his pocket for his cell phone and called Mr. Waggoner. "Hello, Mr. Waggoner. This is Bob from the youth group at church. We are planning a Halloween party and need a hay wagon and a team of horses for a hay ride. Would you be willing to help us out?"

"Sure, Bob. What date would you want me?"

"Are you available the last Friday in October?"

"I have nothing scheduled for that date. I'll put your group down for a hay ride. Will the group come to my farm or would I need to come to the church?"

"One minute, please, while I ask Joe about where to meet you."

"Joe," asked Bob, "Mr. Waggoner wants to know if we would meet at his farm or if he needs to come to the church."

"We'll meet him at his farm."

"We'll drive the group out to your farm before the hay ride," said Bob.

"Thanks, I appreciate that and thanks for thinking of me," said Mr. Waggoner.

"Oh, good," said Sally, "I like hay rides. I like to snuggle down into the hay; it smells so good, and talking with friends makes it all the more enjoyable. Of course I'll have to take a bath and wash my hair later at home, but the time with friends and the talking makes the hay in my hair and clothing all the more worthwhile."

"Wouldn't it be fun to have a hay fight?" said Bob.

Sally narrowed her eyes, looked at Bob and glared at him.

"If Bob starts throwing hay I hope, Sara, you and Lynn will help me hold him down so I can stuff some hay down the back of his shirt."

"I may have to get back at you," said Bob laughing.

"Just how will you do that?" laughed Sally.

"I have some plans I won't tell you about," Bob said with a snicker.

Everyone laughed. "This sounds like fun, just make sure no one is injured," Nina said.

"I like the one called pin the hat on the scarecrow, even if Lynn misses the entire board," giggled Sara with a huge smile.

"It sounds like a good game with a lot of laughs," chuckled Lynn. "Stay away from the board so you don't end up wearing the hat, Sara."

Nina added put the hat on the scarecrow game on her list. "We will need someone to make a scarecrow. Lynn, Bob, I appoint the two of you to do that task. Bring the gentleman here to the house when it is finished.

"We will do that," said both Lynn and Bob.

"Are we finished planning?" asked Joe.

"Oh, no" replied Bob. "We still have the most important part of the party night to plan."

"And what part of the party night is that, as if I didn't know?" asked Sara.

"The food," stated Bob.

Sara, Sally, and Nina began to laugh. "You men always have food on your minds," said the girls.

"What else is important? Besides growing boys need their food," said Bob.

"I'll admit, both of you young men look like you don't get enough to eat," laughed Sally.

"My sisters don't eat much, they are afraid they'll gain an ounce. I, however, have a hollow stomach that empties as fast as I fill it," said Bob.

"Okay," said Nina, "what would you like to eat after the hay ride?"

"How about hamburgers, hot dogs, and chips, along with cake and ice cream?"

Everyone laughed.

"We need to be careful; if we have hot dogs you'll want to roast them over a fire and that means gathering wood, wiener forks, or long sticks. I want no injuries," said Joe. "I would suggest that we have pizza and sodas instead. We could all come here after the hay ride and play games. We could build a small fire in my fire pit so people can stay warm if the night becomes cold. Maybe some of the group

---

---

members could make pizzas and others could see about the soft drinks."

"Is there enough money in the group treasury to purchase the needed materials?" asked Sara.

"We have close to $100 in the treasury. If we are careful and shop wisely we should have enough money. We have three or four meetings and if we announce that we need larger offerings and why we need them, we could add $30 or $40 to the treasury," said Nina. "We should give Mr. Waggoner something for the use of his horses and wagon."

"Lynn, you and Bob ask a couple more boys to help get the soft drinks. Sara, you and Sally ask some girls to help you purchase supplies and make the pizzas. If you make them the Saturday before the party, they could be frozen until party time so we only need to bake them," said Nina.

"This sounds like a fun time," said Lynn to the others. I'm glad we were asked to help with the planning. Now if we could just make the time go faster until the party."

"Why?" asked Nina with a twinkle in her eye. "I'm hungry already and I have to wait a whole week." A hay ride makes a guy hungry," agreed Bob, smiling.

"Are you sure you don't have a hollow leg and a turbo drive stomach?" giggled Sally.

"I think you are on to something, Sally. At times both of my legs hurt when I am hungry."

At that Nina laughed and said, "Bob, take your friends home and raid your Mom's refrigerator." The girls just laughed and rolled their

---

eyes as they all walked out of Joe and Nina's back yard and headed home.

"Good bye everyone," called Joe.

"See you Sunday at church," stated Bob smiling. "These guys are fun!" he said to the others.

"You got that right. We really have a good group of kids in the youth group, too," Sally said.

"I agree," Sara said, "we'll have a really fun time at the hay ride."

"Yes, we'll all have a good time. The entire group of us are friends and we all like each other so whatever we do at the hay ride will be considered gentle teasing and no one will go home with hurt feelings.

Forever Hopeful

Chapter Eight

As they left Joe and Nina's home, Lynn and Sara saw Tony and Rachael leave Hardee's and begin riding their bikes toward them. Tony spoke loud enough so everyone near them could hear them speaking.

"Look at that, Rachael, Lynn and Sara riding their bikes together. They study together after school almost every night at the public library and sometimes on Saturday too. I'll bet they are dating."

"Could be," said Rachael, "They both think they're so smart, and that Sara is so pretty and thin."

"I know. Lynn is no good at sports, but he does well in school. Have you noticed how he holds his head to one side in class? I wonder if he is copying from his neighbor. Sara is so smart, and she sits right across the aisle from Lynn in two classes."

"I don't think he's copying or cheating, Tony. He is too smart to need to do any of those things. I know he is blind in one eye and he holds his head to one side so he can see the paper or book he is working from."

"Well, Rachael, it is interesting that they spend so much time together. I do think they are dating. Let's catch up to them and give them a bad time," said Tony.

"Tony, leave them alone," said Rachael.

"No. It is so much fun to tease Lynn; he hardly ever says anything back."

"That's because he is so shy."

"I'm going to give him a bad time anyway." Peddling faster on their bikes, Tony and Rachael soon caught up to Lynn and Sara.

Lynn moaned and rolled his eyes up into his forehead. *Here come Tony and Rachael, and he has his "I'm going to give you a bad time" look on his face. I wonder what he is up to this time.* Tony rode his bike around Lynn's and Sara's bikes, forcing them to stop to avoid a wreck.

"Well, look here, Rachael, we have Lynn and Sara out riding their bikes together. Almost every night they study at the public library. Let me see, could they be dating each other? Yep, that's it. Why else would they spend so much time together?"

"Well, Tony, Sara has that 'I'm in love' look on her face."

"Tony, we are not in love. We are just friends who enjoy each other's company," said Lynn.

"I think you two are in love," said Tony.

"Tony, don't you have anything better to do than bugging other people?" asked Sara.

"I'm just stating the obvious," said Tony.

"Obvious is a pretty big word for you, Tony. Do you know what it means?"

"No, but it makes me sound like I have brains."

"Just as I thought. Tony, if you would spend more time on your school assignments you'd know what obvious means. But, I don't want to obfuscate you, so just go away," said Sara.

"Obfus-- what? Speak plain English, or does being in love do that to you?" said Rachael. "Let's go Tony."

"Good for you, Sara," said Lynn after Tony and Rachael had gone.

"You got him all confused just like obfuscate means. I really do feel sad about Tony. He could be an excellent student as well as athlete if he would just try with his school work. I'm going to be kind to him; maybe he'll become as good a student as he is an athlete."

Tony and Rachael soon came back and began to ride in circles around Lynn and Sara. Lynn told Sara to move to the side, and he watched as Tony kept riding his bicycle around Lynn in ever shrinking circles. Sara and Rachael told him to stop. Tony just laughed at the girls and at Lynn.

"Tony, stop! you are going to cause an accident and hurt someone," begged Rachael.

"Not me," said Tony. "If the loser here doesn't know enough to get out of my way, he deserves to be hurt."

"Tony, you mean you would purposely hurt Lynn?" exclaimed Sara.

"Like I said, if he doesn't know enough to get out of my way, he deserves to be hurt."

"Tony, stop being a bully," said Rachael. Tony kept riding around Lynn, smiling, and challenged Lynn to make him stop riding.

"Come on loser, make me stop."

"Tony, if this is your idea of fun, you are the loser, not me," said Lynn.

"Ho, ho, the dud spoke to me, even dared to call me a loser."

"Tony, watch out for that loose gravel. Tony," Rachael screamed, "stop this foolishness."

Just then Tony's bike hit the patch of loose gravel sending him flying off his bike and into Lynn. Lynn fell of his bike as a result of the impact and fell spread eagle onto the gravel and pavement sliding several feet. Sara and Rachael screamed and rushed to Lynn's side and helped him sit up.

"Lynn, are you hurt?" asked Rachael. Then she and Sara both noticed the crimson stain of blood spreading on his shirt, knees, and his chin.

"Tony, you've hurt Lynn," said Sara.

"It's probably just a small scratch. He'll be alright."

Lynn stared at Tony.

"Sara," whispered Rachael, "did you notice how Lynn looked at Tony? I've never seen his eyes so black or his hands clenched so tight."

"I know. I saw that look on his face as well as you. I've never seen Lynn so angry. He doesn't say anything though."

"With all this blood it's more than just a scratch," exclaimed Rachael.

"Tony, I think your bullying of Lynn has gone too far," cried Sara.

"Oh, he'll be alright, stop worrying and making a big deal of nothing."

"Do you call all this blood nothing?" Sara said. "Rachael help me with Lynn."

Carefully they helped Lynn stand up.

"Besides the blood on your shirt, slacks, and chin, do you hurt anywhere else? asked Rachael.

"I'm okay, I just need to go home and clean up, change clothes, and see about this bleeding."

Sara and Rachael helped Lynn walk slowly to his bicycle. Standing it up, Lynn began to walk home with Sara beside him.

"Lynn, I'm so sorry and I'm so proud of you for not doing any fighting with Tony or saying anything mean to him."

"Thank you, Sara. I had to bite my tongue to keep from saying anything more than what I did. There were plenty of thoughts in my mind that I could have said, but thank God He helped me not to say them. Well, here we are at my house. Thanks for your help, Sara. You truly are a friend in deed."

"Lynn, what are your favorite cookies?" asked Sara. "Chocolate chip and salted peanut cookies are my favorites. "I'll make some for you and bring them tonight about 8 o'clock." "I may not look beautiful or handsome, but you will be welcome, Sara."

Lynn hobbled into the house and went to the bathroom. Thankfully his mother and Dad were not at home. He shed his clothing and put them in the bathtub. The knee and skin on his right leg were all scratched up. His chest and right arm were still seeping a little blood, but his chin had stopped bleeding. Carefully he cleansed his wounds with soap and water and applied an antibiotic cream.

Taking a few large squares of gauze he taped them over his arm, chest, knee and right leg. The cut on his chin appeared smaller than he first thought, so he just applied some antibiotic cream to a bandage. He soaked the clothes in cold water in the tub, so the blood wouldn't stain, then dressed and waited for his Mother and Dad to come home.

When his dad walked in the door, he asked, "Lynn, what happened to you?"

"Well, Dad, I was run into by Tony and I fell and slid about five feet on some loose gravel. I cleaned myself up, and put on some antibiotic cream and bandages. I'll be alright."

At that moment his mom walked into the room. Seeing Lynn's bandage on his chin, she screamed, "Lynn, what happened to you?"

"Just a bike accident, Mom. I'll be fine. My body will heal."

"How did it happen?"

"Tony ran into me and I fell onto some loose gravel."

"I think we should call the police and have Tony arrested."

"No, Mom, it was an accident."

"Honey, stop over reacting. He says it was an accident and Lynn will heal with time. Now go deal with dinner."

"I still think Tony should be arrested." Lynn's mother cried and she stomped her foot.

Just then the doorbell rang and Lynn's dad went to answer the bell. When he opened the door, he found Sara with a box decorated with a blue bow. "Hi, Sara; come in. I know you are here to see Lynn, and not me. What do you have in the box?"

"I have some cookies for Lynn. If you talk nice to him, I think he'll share with you."

"I hope so; the cookies smell delicious," Lynn's dad smiled. "Lynn is in the den."

"Thank you."

The next few days in school, boys would clap Lynn on the shoulder and ask, "How is Sara?" Others would say, "Hi, lover boy." Girls would tell Sara that being in love made her smile more and she certainly looked happier. Looking at Lynn, several classmates asked, "What happened to you?"

Just a bike accident," Lynn answered. After school, Lynn decided to call Sara. *Tony is up to his usual self again. I don't want Sara hurt.*
I'm going to call her and ask to meet with her and her parents to discuss this problem. Maybe they can give me some insight. I know so little about girls and do not understand them or how she is reacting to all of this. I'm going to call right now and see if we can talk and resolve this tonight.

Going to the phone, Lynn dialed the number of Sara's home.

"Hello, this is Sara speaking."

"Hello, Sara, this is Lynn."

"Hi, Lynn how are you?"

"I'm confused and miserable, Sara. May I come to your house and visit with both you and your parents for a few minutes?"

"Well, yes, is something wrong?"

"I need some advice about our friendship, Sara, and I want your parents and your opinions about my questions."

"I'll ask my parents, hold on for a minute. Mom, Dad, Lynn wants to come and discuss some questions with us."

"Sure, honey girl, Lynn is welcome at our home," said her father.

"Will you be coming right away, Lynn?'

"Yes, Sara, I'll be there in about 10 minutes."

"Okay, good bye."

"Did Lynn say what his questions are?" asked Sara's mother.

"No, but he sounded so worried."

Soon the doorbell rang and Mr. Brown opened the door. He asked Lynn to follow him into the living room, and invited him to sit in a big comfortable chair.

"Thank you for allowing me to come on such a short notice," said Lynn.

"That's quite all right, Lynn, you are welcome in our home. You and Sara have become good friends and we are glad she chose a fine young man as you are for a friend."

"Sara is a nice young lady and I enjoy her friendship."

"So, Lynn, Sara said you had some questions you wanted to discuss with us. Please tell us what they are."

"Well, Sir and Ma'am, I think the world of Sara and I do not want to see her hurt. There are some students at school who are spreading rumors about Sara and me. They say that we are dating each other and in love with each other. I do like her, but my only interest in Sara is friendship. If our studying together is going to hurt her reputation, then I think we should stop studying together after school at the library. You continue to study there, Sara, and I'll study at home."

"Oh, Lynn, thank you for caring about me. I value our friendship and I think of you only as a friend in addition to being a gentleman and a very caring person. We are only 15 years old and too young to date. Tony has started these rumors and he is the kind of person who thinks it is fun to make others feel miserable. I think he is jealous of our friendship and wishes he had a friend as you and I have. There is nothing we can do to stop these rumors and ending our friendship will not help. If we continue to act in a responsible manner and treat each other and others with respect, I think the rumors will soon stop."

"Sara is right, Lynn. You are a fine young man and we are proud to have you as Sara's friend. Continue to act in a responsible manner and treat each other and your classmates with respect and this will soon die away."

"I appreciate your kind words but Sara, I don't understand girls. Doesn't this hurt you, and make you feel bad? If we ended our friendship wouldn't the problem disappear?"

"Lynn, I care about you as a person. I'm sad to see you hurting like this. Our friendship means a lot to me. These rumors are only temporary. Our friendship is something I had always dreamed of. A person I could do things with, laugh with, someone who had nearly the same goals and feelings I do. I want lots of friends like you, a friendship that lasts for years and years. I think you want the same thing, Lynn."

"I do, Sara, I want lots of friends like you."

"Well then, Lynn, let's stay friends and continue to study together after school, and still be part of the youth group at church."

"Mom and Dad, what do you think about our conclusion?"

"We both think you are wise beyond your 15 years. We are proud of our daughter and of you Lynn. You are always welcome here and we trust you with our daughter."

"Thank you, sir, and ma'am. I appreciate your kindness and value your opinion of me.

Lynn rode his bike home. He rode slowly thinking about his conversation with Sara and her parents . *I'm so happy that they trust me and that Sara values our friendship so much. I do too. Tony can really be a pain sometimes, but I think that deep down inside is a good person trying to come to the surface. I think that if I react with kindness and respect to his teasing and negative comments he will change his attitude and habits.*

When he arrived at home, Lynn parked his bike in the garage and went to his room. "Dear Father in heaven," he prayed, "please help me to be kind and respectful to Tony. You know him better than I. I think there is a lot of good in Tony. I think part of his problem is that he wants friends, but doesn't know how to be a friend. Maybe, just maybe, I can lead him to you. Dear Father, work in his heart. Thank you for what you've done for me. In Jesus name. Amen.

Forever Hopeful

Chapter Nine

Lynn spent much more time in prayer about Tony and Rachael that night after meeting with Sara and her parents.

"Dear Father in heaven, I'm so concerned about Tony and

Rachael. Neither one seems to be interested in you. Please send your Holy Spirit into their lives and show them their need for you and salvation. If it is your will, use me to lead the two of them to you so that they want you to save their souls. I know Tony antagonizes me, but you love him and Rachael as much as you love me. Give me the opportunity to speak with Tony and Rachael about you and please give me the words to say that will help him and Rachael see their need for you and ask you to inhabit their lives. In Jesus' name, Amen."

The next day at school Lynn was able to talk with Sara as they quietly sat in a corner and ate their lunches.

"Sara, what do you think about inviting Tony and Rachael to come

more regularly to the youth group at church? They've been there once or twice. If they come regularly they would get acquainted with some good kids and hopefully they might come to believe in God and Jesus."

"Good idea, Lynn, I'll talk to Rachael, you talk to Tony."

"Sara, I need your prayer support, also."

"About what, Lynn? You seem so serious."

"I am, Sara. I want to ask Tony and Rachael to come to the hay ride. I think Tony would like to have friends, but doesn't know how to make a friend or to keep a friend. I think the same of Rachael."

"Do you think that is wise, Lynn? Tony and Rachael are rough people."

"I know. But I also know God loves Tony and Rachael as much as He loves you and me. I feel that I, we, are the hands, feet, and voice of the Lord to tell others about Him. I think God expects us to tell others about Him and, in this case, I feel it's you and me."

"All right, Lynn, I'll be glad to pray for Tony and Rachael to yield to Christ and I'll also pray for God to give us the right words to say. Let's pray right now."

"Dear Jesus, we have a burden for the souls of Tony and Rachael. Please work in their hearts, softening them to yourself and give us the words to speak to them so that they see their need for you and salvation. We do not want to do anything that will drive them away from you. In Jesus' name, Amen."

"Thank you, Sara; I knew I could count on you for your help

Lynn and Sara had just finished their lunches when the bell rang warning them they had five minutes before their next class. "Have a good afternoon, Sara, I'll see you at the public library to study after school."

"You have a good afternoon too, Lynn."

Between classes, Lynn saw Tony and invited him to come with him to the church youth group meeting on Sunday evening.

"I don't care to go to a stuffy old youth group meeting, and sing a bunch of hymns that were written 300 years ago."

"Oh, Tony, we do sing some hymns, but also some more modern Christian music and have a Bible lesson."

"I'd rather play football, or basketball, maybe baseball. Count me out."

Later Lynn said to Sara, "I saw Tony between classes and invited him to the youth group, but he said he'd rather play sports,"

"I'm sorry, Lynn. Don't give up, these things take time. He's proud of his athletic ability and talent. Praise his skills in sports next time you see him and tell him that half of the football team is part of the youth group."

"Good idea, Sara, I'll do that. Have you talked to Rachael yet?"

"No, I haven't seen her yet today. Maybe I'll call her tonight and invite her to the youth group after we study at the library."

During the next few days, Lynn saw Tony often and praised and complimented Tony on his skills in sports. "I saw you during the football game last Friday night. The way you faked out the opposing tackle on your touchdown run was awesome. Then there was the tackle you made that stopped the opposing team's running back to save a touchdown. Wow that was really good."

"Careful, Lynn, it might go to my head. Don't you wish you could be a better athlete and as good as me?"

"Yes, Tony, I wish I could be a better athlete."

"I'll coach you Lynn."

"I'd like that and appreciate that, Tony. I'd also like it if you would go to the youth group with me. We are going to have a hay ride at our next party. I think you'd enjoy that. Did you know, Tony, that half of the football team are members of our youth group?"

"Really? I didn't know that. If I went I'd at least know more people than just you and Sara."

"That's right, Tony, and you'd see that Christian kids don't just sit around singing hymns that are over 300 years old. They want to have good clean fun just like you do."

"Okay, you talked me into it. I'll go if Rachael will go with me."

"Tony, are you becoming sweet on Rachael and falling in love with her? I see you two together a lot of the time."

"I guess I deserved that, Lynn. No, I am not sweet on Rachael; she is just a good friend like you are with Sara."

"Good, Tony, I'm glad you have a friend, Youth group starts at 6:00 P.M. on Sunday night. May I stop at your house and walk with you? I'll introduce you to some of the guys and girls."

At school the next week word soon circulated that Tony was going on the hay ride.

"Hey guys, I hear Tony is going on the hay ride," said Jim.

"No, really?" said Marlene.

"Yes, Lynn invited him to come and see that Christian kids have fun too. Let's show him that we are not a stuffy bunch of strange people who sit around and sing 300 year old hymns," Tom said.

"I agree to that," said Susan. "I'm glad he is coming. I think he could be a really fine person. Maybe we can help him turn his life around, change his attitude from sour to sweet, and improve his school grades."

"I don't know if I like Tony coming to the youth group hay ride. He is a bully and rough person. He could cause trouble," Eric said.

"Friends, let's all pray for Tony that God will change his life," said Jim.

"Hello, Tony, we hear you are going on the hay ride. We're glad to have you. Get ready for a good time," said Tom.

"Are you going to bring Rachael?" asked Marlene.

"Yes, she agreed to come with me."

"Good. Rachael, we'll help clue you in on the activities," said several girls.

"Hey guys, thanks for praying for Tony, and offering to help Rachael," said Lynn.

"Oh, Lynn," said Sara, "you may be a quiet person but you are one excellent friend. I admire you for the way you've included Tony after the way he has treated you all these years,"

"Sara, God loves Tony and I think of him as a good person. His goodness is buried deep inside. His goodness has been covered up too long. I see him as a future friend. Kindness wins more friends than vengeance or angry comments back to an antagonist. I know I haven't said much when Tony pesters me, but I think that deep down inside there is a good person trying to surface. I'd rather win a friend than make an enemy."

"Lynn, you are someone special. I am proud to call you my friend."

"I am proud to call you my friend as well, Sara. You too are someone special. Let's make this hay ride one no one will ever forget."

Forever Hopeful

Chapter Ten

"Sara, what do you know about Tony and Rachael? I don't know much about either one of them."

"Okay, Lynn, let's talk about Tony first. We know he likes sports, and he is a good player. We also know he likes malts, burgers, and fries. We know he is not fond of school; he goes only because he is required to be there. We know he can be a pain, teasing people about things that hurt them. What is his home life like? Why does he act like he does? We only know surface things about him, nothing really in depth. He has few friends besides Rachael."

"Now let's talk about Rachael. Sara, it's your turn, since you are a girl."

"Well, she is sad most of the time, I rarely see her smile. She eats the wrong kinds of foods which is probably the cause of her complexion problem and weight gain. She does okay in school, but could do better. She has few friends which I think is the reason for her sadness. We know nothing about her family or her home life. I think both Tony and Rachael would like more friends but I think they don't know how to go about making and keeping friends."

"So, how can we help both of them?" asked Lynn.

"First, they have to want help," said Sara. "We can't force the help on them."

"Keep talking, Sara, how do we make them want help?"

"As you said, Lynn, we treat them with kindness and respect. The girls in the youth group can help Rachael, the boys help Tony."

"Good plan, Sara, what items do you think we should discuss with them?"

"We need to discuss their attitude toward school, help them improve their study skills and habits. We also need to discuss their relationship with other persons, to tone down their conversations from critical criticism to being more supportive and kind. We also need to understand, ourselves, that there will be times when they fall back into their old behaviors even if they become Christians. We need to bring them back to their new behavior with kindness and love."

"This hay ride is going to be a new experience for them. Lynn, let's you and I walk to Tony's home and then to Rachael's home and walk with them to the church. We can talk about what they can expect on the hay ride, including the singing, teasing, and general conversation."

"Good ideas, Sara. Why don't you call Rachael tonight and I'll call Tony. We'll tell them we'll pick them up a half hour before the start of the hay ride and walk to church with them. We can introduce them to the sponsors and kids who go to other schools. And, Sara, pray that God will help us know what to say to Tony and Rachael and that we'll have a good time on the hay ride."

Soon the day for the hay ride came and all the members of the group excitedly talked about the ride. "Mary Ann," said Tom," your hair is always so nice, but I think it would look better with some hay in it."

"You do that, Tom, and I'll get some of my girlfriends to hold you down while I stuff hay down your back. Then you can itch and scratch all night," Mary Ann laughed.

"Tony, you're an excellent athlete, do you think you can run faster than the horses?" Bob asked.

"No problem, it won't even be a contest," Tony answered.

"But remember, Tony, the horses have four legs and you only have two, you'll have to use twice as much energy as the horses."

"No, it will only take half the energy for me as it does the horses," Tony laughed.

"Everyone into the church vans," announced Joe and Nina. "It is time to go to Mr. Waggoner's farm for the hay ride."

With cheers all around the youth group loaded the vans and after a five mile ride arrived at the Waggoner farm.

"Tony and Rachael, I'd like for you to meet our group sponsors, Joe and Nina a really nice couple of people who love teenagers," Lynn said.

"Hi Tony, hi Rachael, we like to have new people come on our outings. We want you to have a good time tonight. Join in the fun and teasing. Come back to meet with our group on Sunday night. You'll be most welcome. Stick with Lynn and Sara. They'll help you get acquainted with all the kids in the group."

"Thanks for asking us and allowing us to come on this outing," Rachael said.

"Lynn and Sara, introduce them to the kids from schools other than your own," Nina said.

"We will do that, Nina," Sara said.

"First, Tony, you're an excellent athlete. I'd like to introduce you to someone you will no doubt meet on a basketball court soon. This tall young man is Doug, but we call him Stretch because he stands about 6'6" and is still growing," Lynn said.

"Hi, short stuff, how's the weather down there?" Stretch said.

"Hello yourself, I'm glad to meet you," Tony replied.

"Yeah, Stretch, let us know when it starts to rain so we can get under cover before we're all wet like you," Mary Ann said.

Soon the laughter and good-natured teasing was interrupted by the people on the back of the hay rack singing contemporary Christian music. "Come on, you guys," said Joe, "let's join the others on the hay rack." Soon, with a full load, the horses began pulling the rack down the lane.

"Tom, put that hay down." Tom just smiled and kept crawling toward Mary Ann. "Girls, keep him away from me." She laughed.

"Sure, Mary Ann. We're glad to help." Soon four girls had Tom under control and he couldn't move his arms or legs.

"Help me, guys, I'm being held captive by four pretty girls," Tom moaned.

"Oh, you poor fellow, you look like you are really enjoying being held down by four pretty girls," several boys said.

"I am, but don't tell them. I don't want them to stop."

"Mary Ann, would you like to stuff some hay down his back while we have him in this helpless state?" laughed the girls.

"Sure thing, keep him pinned down while I gather some hay," Mary Ann laughed.

"You won't even get close to Tom," said Stretch. "I'll wrap my arms around your shoulders and pick you up so you can see what the weather is like at my level." With that he picked up a laughing Mary Ann. He held her in his arms like a baby while she kicked her legs.

Joe and Nina laughed and said, "You'd better let Tom go although He seems to be enjoying being held down by four girls and Mary Ann is enjoying being held by Stretch."

Everyone laughed as Mary Ann and Tom each tossed a hand full of hay at each other, purposely missing the other person, exchanging smiles and laughter.

"I'm getting cold," said Susan. Some of you girls sit close by me and help me warm up."

"Scoop some hay over your legs; that will help you keep warm."

"We'll help," said several girls and fellows and soon Susan was nearly covered with hay.

"Enough, enough," laughed Susan, I'll be warm now. Thanks friends, for your kind help."

"We'll turn back now, we've been riding for an hour and it will take us an hour to arrive back at the farm," said Mr. Waggoner.

"Aw" raised the chorus of teenage voices, "we're just starting to have fun."

"I know. You are good kids and I enjoy having you at my farm. Time flies when you're having fun. My wife has hot chocolate and donuts waiting for you at the farm house."

Again cheers erupted from the hay rack. "Thank you, Mr. Waggoner, for taking us on the hay ride. Three cheers for Mr. Waggoner. Hip hip hooray, hip hip hooray, hip hip hooray," chorused the teenagers. Joe very carefully stood up and held onto the back fence of the hay rack.

"While we are enjoying the hot chocolate and donuts, we will give you a chance to give a testimony about how God has helped you lately. I've heard you discussing school, school projects, homework, and science fair projects. After listening, I'm glad I've graduated. Those teachers are working you quite hard."

That statement caused a series of groans. Tony added, "Lynn and Sara enjoy the research. It gives them an excuse to study together on Saturdays at the public library."

"Maybe more of us should do that. No wonder they're so smart," shouted Tom.

"Sure, join us, the more the merrier," said Sara. "There's lots of room and the librarians are lots of help. But you must be quiet. A library is like a study hall at school, no one talks above a whisper, or you'll be sent home."

"Phooey," said Stretch, Dave and Tom, "librarians are too strict."

When they arrived at the farm, the youth group jumped off the wagon and walked toward Mrs. Waggoner who laid out paper plates, cups, and donuts. "Come to me by the camp stove for your hot chocolate. Eat donuts and drink until it is all gone. Girls, first in line. Those boys suffering from hollow leg syndrome will eat everything and leave nothing for the girls."

"What is hollow leg syndrome?" asked Rachael.

Mary Ann said, "That's just a joke. Boys this age are always hungry and they can eat so much and never gain weight. So we say they must have a hollow leg and that is where all the food goes, into a hollow leg."

"Oh," said Rachael, "I don't have any brothers."

"I do," said Mary Ann, "three of them, and there are never any leftovers after a meal at my house. If I don't serve myself first, I don't get much to eat."

"Gather 'round kids. It's testimony time," said Joe. "Who wants to be first?"

Lynn stood up. "God has blessed me with lots of friends. I enjoy school and learning. With God's help, because of God's help, I am what I am."

Sara stood up. "God has blessed me with loving parents, and caring friends."

Mary Ann rose. "I thank God for all of you as friends too, even Tom. I know he was only teasing about the hay in my hair."

At last Tom stood up. "I thank God for giving me such good friends who understand my teasing as only fun." Walking over toward Mary Ann, he put his arm around her shoulder." I do have a present for you Mary Ann." Reaching into his pocket he pulled out a handful of hay.

"Would you like this present in your hair or in your hand?"

Everyone roared with laughter as Mary Ann said, "I'd like it on the ground, Tom. But I'll always treasure this little bit of hay."

"Okay," said Nina, it's time to go back to church. Your parents are waiting for you. Everyone tell Mr. and Mrs. Waggoner thank you for the hay ride and food."

"Thank you," the youth group chorused.

"Tony, Rachael, sit by Sara and me on the ride back to church," said Lynn.

"Why?" asked Tony.

"We want to invite you to our youth group meeting on Sunday night and we can talk about the hay ride on the way home."

"I did have a good time tonight," admitted Tony. "It turned out better than I expected. I thought Christian kids were stuffy and boring, but you guys know how to have fun."

"I enjoyed myself too," said Rachael. "You make life enjoyable. Thank you."

Forever Hopeful

Chapter Eleven

Sara and Lynn walked with Tony and Rachael from church to their homes. All four of them expressed happiness about the hay ride and the enjoyable time they experienced.

"Tony and Rachael, would you like to come to our youth group meeting Sunday night? Lynn asked.

"What time does the meeting start and how long does it last? What do you do at the meetings?" asked Rachael. "Do the guys and girls sit together or do they separate to the sides of the room?" Rachael asked.

"The meeting starts at 6:30 P. M. and ends at 7:30 P. M." Sara said.

"We usually sing a song or two, listen to a Bible story, have a snack and after the meeting talk about anything," Lynn said.

"Sometimes, after the meeting the girls get together to one side of the room and talk about girl things," Sara said.

"The boys talk about school, sports, girls and cars," Lynn said.

"Okay, pick me up, I have some questions I'd like to ask the girls and Nina," Rachael said.

"I'd like to talk about cars and sports," Tony said.

"Good, we'll pick you up about 6:00 PM and walk over to the church. I'm glad the two of you are willing to come with us," Lynn said.

Soon they reached the home of Rachael and then Tony's home. Continuing on toward their own homes, Lynn and Sara discussed the hay ride and discussion of their friends.

"Sara, we need to talk to God again and thank Him for helping us to have a good time tonight and for Tony and Rachael being willing to come to the youth group meeting on Sunday night."

"I agree, Lynn, let's sit on my parent's front porch and pray."

"Good idea, Sara."

After sitting down in separate chairs Lynn began to pray. "Dear Father, you know all things. You know the end from the beginning in all things that concern us. We've invited Tony and Rachael to our youth group meeting at church. We want both of them to come to know you as Lord and Savior of their lives. We also want to help Tony be a friendlier person and Rachael to improve her appearance. We feel that deep down inside they are good kids. Give us and the rest of the kids in the group the words to say to encourage them to seek you and become the kind of people they can become. We love them as you love them. In Jesus name we pray, Amen."

Sara smiled and said, "That is the same prayer I was going to pray.

Dear Father, I echo Lynn's prayer and to his prayer I add my girl's point of view. Most girls want to be pretty and, if Rachael will let us, the girls in the youth group can help her. Help her to let us do what we can to help her. In Jesus name, I pray, Amen."

At the end of Sara's prayer the porch light came on and Sara said, "Hi, Daddy."

"I knew it was you and Lynn out here. I listened to you praying and I agree with your prayers. Sara, how did you know it was me?"

Sara began to giggle, "I peeked while Lynn was praying and I saw you sitting by the window."

"You need to come in now, Sara; you have church and Sunday school tomorrow. Lynn's Dad called and asked if he was here. I told him you were on the front porch praying and he said, "Tell Lynn to come home when they are finished.""

"I'm going," Lynn said. "Good night Mr. Brown. Good night, Sara. I'll see all of you in church tomorrow. Good night Mrs. Brown, I know you are in the living room."

"Lynn you are such a delight," Mrs. Brown laughed. Sara giggled quietly too and Mr. Brown just smiled.

"Come again, Lynn," Mrs. Brown said.

`Lynn walked home feeling good inside. He thanked God for his friendship with Sara and the other people in the youth group. Upon arriving home he looked at his father with a smile on his face. "Dad, how did you know I would be at Sara's house?"

"Simple son, I know you and Sara are friends, good friends. She is a wonderful person and I am happy she is your friend. You spend a lot of time helping each other study and at youth group. If you are not with her at church, school, or the library, I know you'll be with Sara somewhere.

"I wish you would spend more time at home, Lynn. I don't get to see you much," his mother said.

"Mom, you know I'm busy with school and church. I want to earn good grades so I can maybe earn a college scholarship. I'll tell you what, I'll spend tomorrow afternoon here at home with you and Dad. Okay, Mom?"

"I can't Lynn. I have my ladies group from church coming for tea tomorrow afternoon."

The next morning Lynn and his parents went to church and Sunday school. He saw many of his school class mates. He told them Tony and Rachael made plans to come to the youth group meeting that night. "Let's all be kind to Tony and Rachael. I know Tony is a bit negative, but maybe if we show them God's love through us we can help both change their life styles."

"Oh, good," several chorused.

Just then Sara walked up. "Hi, everyone. What are we talking about?"

"Lynn just told us Tony and Rachael are coming tonight. I'd like to know Rachael better. She seems so withdrawn like she wishes she had more friends," Barbara said.

"Let's treat them with kindness and respect. If you girls would get Rachael off to one side maybe she would open up a bit and let you in on some of her thoughts and wishes," said Lynn.

"We guys will talk to Tony.

"Sounds good," chorused everyone.

That afternoon Lynn spent time in his bedroom studying to complete his homework assignments and took his trombone to the garage to practice.

Checking his watch he noticed the time was nearing 6:00 o'clock. He packed up his instrument, music, and music stand and returned them to his room. He told his parents he was leaving for church and the youth group meeting.

Knocking on the front door of Sara's home he waited until her Mother opened the door and invited him in. "Sara is ready and here she comes down the hall." She was dressed in a gray flannel pleated

---

skirt and royal blue sweater over a white blouse. She smiled and said, "Hello, Lynn."

"Mom, pray for us and ask God to open Tony and Rachael's hearts to the gospel tonight."

"I will, honey. I'm so proud of you. Have a good time."

"Thanks. Good bye, Mom."

While walking to Tony's house and then to Rachael's house, Lynn didn't say much.

"You are very quiet tonight, Lynn."

"Yes, I'm sorry. I'm trying to think about what I can say to Tony to encourage him to think about his relationship to God. I so much want him to see that God loves him and wants to give him His best. I want that for Rachael, too. I still think there is really a nice person inside each one of them trying to rise to the surface."

"God will help us," Sara said. Arriving at Tony's house, they heard shouting and crying. Lynn and Sara looked at each other. Lynn walked up to the front door and knocked. Everything became quiet quickly as the shouting and crying stopped. Tony opened the door and hastily stepped out. "Let's go," he said.

"Are you okay, Tony," Lynn asked when they had walked half a block.

"Everything is normal as always."

Rachael sat in a lawn chair waiting for them. Standing up she smiled at Sara and told her how nice she looked.

"Thank you, Rachael. You are so kind."

"You always look so nice, Sara. I wish I could look like you."

"Let's talk sometime, Rachael."

"Girls," said Tony." Clothes seem to be so important to them."

"They are," said Sara. "Girls want to look pretty and clothes help them achieve that goal."

"You do look nice, Sara," Tony said.

"What about Rachael, she looks pretty in her pink dress," Sara said.

"Yeah, now that you mention it she does look pretty in pink," Tony said.

Soon they arrived at church. Because it was meeting time, the church buzzed with the sound of voices and laughter. At 6:30 Joe called the meeting to order. "Find a seat kids, we need to start. "Tom, what is your favorite song?"

"Shine, Jesus, Shine." Nina started to play the melody and soon all were singing.

"Mary Jo, what is your favorite song?"

"Deep River," Mary Jo said.

Nina started to play the piano and all the group sang in quiet reverence.

"Tonight's lesson is called the Roman Road. Take your Bibles please and turn to the book of Romans. If any of you have any questions while we have the lesson, feel free to raise your hand and ask your question. I'll do my bests to answer that question."

"Turn to Romans 3:23." Lynn sat next to Tony and helped him find the correct verse. Sara did the same with Rachael. Finally Joe asked for a volunteer to read the verse out loud. Lynn began. "For all

---

have sinned and come short of the glory of God," (Romans 3:23, NIV).

"That means that all of us fall short of God's standard for right living. Not one of us is free of sin."

"Now turn to Romans 6:23. Someone read please."

Sara began to read, "For the wages of sin is death, but the gift of God is eternal life through Jesus Christ our Lord," (Romans 6:23, NIV).

"God has provided a way that we can avoid the penalty of sin. Jesus paid the penalty and we can go free," Joe said. "Now turn to Romans 5:8. Someone read please."

Tom a huge football player, whom Tony knew, began to read. "But God demonstrates His love toward us, in that while we were still sinners, Christ died for us," (Romans 5:8, NIV).

"Joe, what does commended mean?" Susan asked.

"I'm glad you asked, Susan. It means that God showed His love for us by sending Jesus to die for us while we were still sinners. God offered us the gift of salvation even though we were still deep in sin. It is God's proof of His love for us. God didn't have to love us, He just does."

"Now turn to Romans 10:13. We need another reader."

Barbara began to read, "For everyone who calls upon the name of the Lord will be saved," (Romans 10:13, NIV).

"Does anyone have a question? Joe asked.

"Yes," Tony said. "What does call on the name of the Lord mean?"

"Good question, Tony," said Joe. "I'm going to change the way we have been answering questions now. Does anyone have an answer for Tony?" Tom stood up and said, "It takes faith to pray to God and call on Him. We need to believe He will hear us and answer our prayer request."

Mary Jo stood up and said, "Tom is right; we need to believe God will hear our prayer, but we also need to believe that Jesus' death on the cross paid the penalty for our sins."

Lynn stood up and said, "If you call on the Lord, you are acknowledging that He is God and He can help you."

Sara stood up and said, "I'm thinking of the Bible story of the Publican and the Pharisee. The Publican knelt in a corner of the temple and pleaded with God to forgive his sins. The Pharisee stood where everyone could see him and boasted to God of all the things he had done. The story says that only one of them, the Publican, went home justified before God."

Sally stood up and said, "If we pray, believing in God and ask for forgiveness for our sins and ask Jesus to come and live in our hearts, He will do that and we have His promise of eternal life with Him when we die."

Joe finally answered Tony's question, "It simply means that if you pray to God about anything, He will hear your prayer and answer you."

"Everyone now find Romans 10:9. Will someone read this verse for us? Okay Dave, your turn."

"That if you confess with your mouth, "Jesus is Lord," and believe in your heart that God raised Him from the dead, you will be saved," (Romans 10:9, NIV).

"What does that mean?" asked Rachael.

"It means, Rachael, that if you tell others that Jesus is Lord and believe in your heart that God raised Him from the dead, alive, you are saved."

"Oh, thank you."

"One final verse," said Joe. "Find Romans 8:1."

Sally stood up and began to read. "Therefore, there is now no condemnation for those who are in Christ Jesus." Everyone was quiet for a moment, then Sally shouted, "Praise the Lord, I did what each verse said to do and thank God I am free of sin and guilt. I will go to heaven when I die. It is guaranteed."

As the meeting ended, Tony said, "I had a good time tonight, this group is wonderful."

Lynn asked, "Tony, are you coming back?"

"Yes," said Tony, "if I may."

"Why of course you may." All the fellows had gathered round Lynn and Tony. "You may come every Sunday."

All the girls had gathered around Rachael. Rachael looked at the girls, "I wish I could look like you do," she said.

"What do you mean, Rachael?" Sara asked.

"All of you girls have such clear complexions and none of you are overweight. I wish I could look like you do." With that statement her eyes began to sting and a few tears rolled down her cheeks.

Nina hugged her close and the other girls touched her arms, back and shoulders. "We'll help you if you want us to."

"Yes, I want your help, but why are you doing this?"

"Well, Rachael, we are Christians and we try to follow Jesus teachings. He said, "Do unto others as you would have them do unto you." We want to help you because we love God and He loves us and you, Rachael."

Tony became a regular attender at church along with Rachael." Everyone could see changes come into Tony's behavior and attitude. His grades at school improved and so did his speech and attitude toward others.

Rachael began to lose weight when she stopped drinking sodas and eating so many fatty foods. She learned how to sew and make new clothing for herself.

One day Tony stopped Lynn in the hall after school. "Lynn," he said," why did you invite us on the hay ride and then to your youth group and church? It doesn't make sense after all the cruel statements and put downs I made about you."

"Because, Tony, God commands me to love others: even those who misuse me. I think you are a nice fellow deep inside. I think that nice guy has been trying to rise to the surface, Tony."

"Hmm, do you mean you care about me?"

"Yes, I do, Tony."

Both Tony and Rachael began to think about the way the youth group had treated them and began to want what the group had. "How can we get what they have? We'll have to talk to Sara and Lynn about our questions."

Forever Hopeful

Chapter Twelve

Tuesday of the next week, Tony and Rachael asked, "Lynn, Sara, may we walk with you?

"Sure thing," Lynn said. "We're glad to have you walk with us."

"Is school going better for you, Tony?" asked Sara.

"Since I changed my attitude and try to do better, things at school are much better. I've picked up some new friends and the football coach said if my grades stay up, I'd be welcome at football practice next fall."

"Oh, Tony," said Lynn, Sara, and Rachael, "that would be terrific. With your skill and ability in sports we might win more games."

"Lynn, why don't you come out for football? I'd help you gain some skill."

"Tony, thank you for your offer, but I'd only warm the bench."

"Lynn," said Sara, "I've never known you to back away from any challenge."

"I usually don't, but I'm not big enough for football."

"You could try out for the PAT kicker and kick off position. That player will graduate this next spring. The position will be wide open."

"Do you think I could develop enough skill, Tony?"

"It will take lots of practice, but you'll never find out if you don't try," said Tony.

"Okay, I'll give it a try. When do we start?"

"If you men are done discussing sports, have you noticed Rachael? She has a clearer complexion and a new outfit on today. You really look nice, Rachael," said Sara.

"Thank you, Sara."

"You certainly do," said Tony. "I'm glad you're my friend, Rachael. What have you done to look so good?"

"Thanks, Tony. The girls and Nina at church have helped me a lot. I've changed what I eat and drink, exercise more, and learned to sew clothing."

"You look nice," said Lynn. "Tony, you asked if you and Rachael could walk with Sara and me. You must have a reason for asking. What is on your mind?"

"Well, I've noticed that the people in the youth group are different from many of the other students at school. What makes you different and why?"

"Rachael, are you wondering and asking the same question?" asked Sara.

"Yes, Sara, I am. Tony and I were not kind to you. I was so envious of your looks and friendship with Lynn. Yet, you treat us with respect and kindness. Why? What do we have to do to be like you?"

"Rachael," answered Sara, "we treat you and Tony the way we do because we are Christians. We follow Jesus Christ. He treated everyone with love and compassion, even those persons who crucified Him. Jesus told us to, "Do for others what you would want them to do for you." Matthew 7:12, (ERV).

"Tony and Rachael, we love you because God loves you and wants to give you eternal life. He will if you confess you are sinners and ask Him to be your Savior."

"Is that all there is to becoming a Christian?" asked Tony. "Don't I have to do something, join a group, pay some money?"

"No, Tony, the gift of salvation is entirely free. All you need to do is believe Jesus is the Son of God, admit you are a sinner in need of forgiveness and ask Jesus to take control of your life," said Lynn.

"Really," said Rachael, "I thought it would be more complicated than that."

"Look, here we are at the church. Would you like to go inside to a quiet room and do this now?" asked Lynn.

"Yes, let's do that."

Lynn and Sara took Tony and Rachael to their Sunday school room and closed the door. They all sat on chairs in a circle.

"Both of you remember the youth group meeting where Joe took us down what is called the Roman Road. Did you understand all of the verses he quoted?" asked Lynn.

"Well, some of the language was difficult to understand," said Tony.

"I have an easier to understand version of the Bible in my back pack. Do you mind if we read those same verses in an easier to understand version?" asked Sara.

"Please do," said Rachael. "Okay, the first verse was Romans 3:23. It reads," 'All have sinned and are not good enough to share God's divine greatness,'" (Romans 3:23, ERV).

"Do you understand that everyone is a sinner, and because of that we cannot relate to God because He is perfect and sinless?" asked Sara.

"Yes," said both Tony and Rachael, "we do understand."

"The second verse was Romans 6:23. It says, "When people sin, they earn what sin pays – death,'" (Romans 6:23, ERV).

"What does that mean?" asked Tony.

"It means, Tony, that if you die without Jesus' forgiveness, you will spend eternity separated from God," said Lynn.

"I don't want that to happen. I want to go to heaven when I die," said Tony.

"I do too," said Rachael.

"The third verse was Romans 5:8. It tells us," 'But Christ died for us while we were still sinners," (Romans 5:8, ERV).

"Do you mean to tell me that Jesus did that even though people were sinners and did not yet believe in Him?" asked Rachael.

"That is correct, Rachael. That is God's love for everyone. He didn't have to do what He did; He did it because He loves us."

"The next verse is Romans 10:13. "Yes, everyone who trusts in the Lord will be saved,'" Romans 10:13, ERV).

"Even me?" asked Tony, astounded. "I've not been kind or loving to anyone, except maybe Rachael, and sometimes I'm not very nice to her. I don't know why she stays with me after the way I treat her sometimes."

"Tony, God will forgive you and anyone else who asks Him. Have you read the Crucifixion story in the Bible? One of the thieves crucified with Jesus asked Him to remember him when he came into

---

His kingdom. Jesus said, "Today you will be with me in paradise." If Jesus could forgive that thief on the cross, who did many sinful things, I am sure he can forgive you for your sins."

"One last verse, and this one is for someone who has accepted Jesus as Savior. It is found in Romans 8:1. It says this, 'So now, anyone who is in Christ Jesus is not judged guilty,'" (Romans 8:1, ERV).

"That means that once you confess your sins and accept Jesus as your Savior, God forgets all of your sins and does not remember them. When you die, you enter heaven as a forgiven sinner," said Sara.

"What do I pray, what words do I use?" asked Tony.

"Tony, just tell God you know you are a sinner and ask Him to come and live in your life," said Lynn.

"Rachael, you can pray the same prayer," said Sara.

Tony and Rachael took each other's hands, closed their eyes and began to pray. "Dear God we both know we are sinners, we confess our sins to you and ask for your forgiveness. Please come and live in our lives and hearts and save our souls, in Jesus name we pray, Amen," Tony prayed.

Then Rachael prayed the same prayer.

"I feel such a sense of peace," said Rachael.

"Me too," said Tony.

Sara hugged Rachael while Lynn shook Tony's hand and patted him on the shoulder.

"Lynn, I'm sorry for the way I treated you in the past. Will you forgive me?" asked Tony.

"Of course I forgive you; you are my brother in Christ."

"Sara, I'm sorry I was so jealous of you," said Rachael. "Please forgive me."

"Of course I forgive you Rachael. You are now my sister in Christ."

"The Bible says there is joy in heaven when one sinner repents. I think there is a real celebration going on now."

Just then Joe, Nina, and the Pastor knocked on the door of the room. "We were about to go home and saw a light down here," said Joe.

"Joe, Nina, Pastor, meet two of God's newest children," said Sara with joy in her voice. "Tell them, Rachael."

"Tony and I just accepted Jesus as our Savior," said a tearful Rachael. "These are tears of joy."

"We are so glad and praise God for you," said Nina.

Lynn said, "May we pray with all of you?"

"Sure," said the pastor of the church. All of them bowed their heads and Lynn began to pray. "Dear Father, you are a great, gracious, and loving God. You know that Sara and I prayed for a long time about Tony and Rachael. We wanted them to learn about you and accept you as Lord and Savior of their lives. Sara and I asked for your help and to give us the words to say to them so they would see their need of you and accept you. Thank you for using us and for working in the hearts of Tony and Rachael. Please keep them close to your side and help them to grow as your children. We praise your name and thank you again for using Sara and I. Amen."

Forever hopeful: Two Years Later:

Chapter Thirteen

"Hey, Lynn, are you going out for football this year?"

Lynn slowly woke up, the dream still lingering in his ears. "I sure wish I could," he whispered.

His mother's voice broke through the early morning stillness.

"Lynn, you need to get up, eat your breakfast and go to buy your school clothes. I'll go with you and help you choose good conservative clothing," said Lynn's mother.

"Mom, I would really rather go with my friends, Tony, Rachael, and Sara. We'll have a good time and I promise I'll not buy anything with alcoholic things on the shirts, or holes in the jeans." He rushed to get dressed.

"Can I trust that they will not try to talk you into something bad?"

"We are all four of us Christians and we try to live for God. You have nothing to worry about. Besides, this will give you time to have your lady friends here for tea, crumpets and jam. We'll be gone most of the morning and a couple of hours this afternoon. When we come here after shopping, we will eat all your leftovers, so be sure to make a lot of food." Lynn smiled at his mother when he arrived downstairs.

"Oh Lynn, at times you are so silly. I can't imagine Tony drinking tea and eating crumpets and jam."

"I'll buy some soft drinks and, just like you and your lady friends, my friends and I will have a good time. Save some crumpets for me

---

and my friends. Tony and I will eat a great number of them, Sara and Rachael maybe two apiece."

"Oh my, Lynn, you really are silly," said his mother.

"I'm going to call Sara now to make arrangements to meet them."

Lynn picked up the phone and dialed Sara's phone number. Soon Sara's Mother answered the phone.

"Hello, Mrs. Brown, is Sara at home?" asked Lynn.

"Lynn, how nice to hear your voice! Yes, she is home. I'll call her to the phone. Sara, honey, Lynn is on the phone wanting to speak with you."

"Hello, Lynn, what a pleasant surprise. What is on your mind?"

"I'm going shopping for school clothes and I'm assuming you will be doing the same. So, I was wondering if we could go together or maybe with Rachael and Tony too."

"This sounds like a fun time. I'll call Rachael and see what her plans for the day are and ask her to call Tony, said Sara.

"Well, Sara, if they can, let's meet at your house at 11 o'clock and after we do our shopping we can come here to my house and clean up all the leftovers from Mothers' tea party this afternoon.

"Oh Lynn, I hope they can go along with us. This sounds like so much fun. Good bye and I'll call Rachael and try to talk her into going shopping. We girls love to shop."

"Yes, I've heard that about girls. Ha Ha."

"Silly boy, I'll get you back for that comment, said Sara laughing.

"Can't wait," said Lynn, laughing too.

At 11 o'clock Lynn walked to Sara's home and saw that Rachael was already on the front porch talking with Sara and her mother.

"I knew it—you girls can't wait to go shopping. I'll bet Rachael is all upset because Tony isn't here yet," said Lynn with a grin on his face.

"Don't even answer him, Rachael," said Sara. "He loves to go shopping with his mother for school clothes. She chooses all the latest styles for him to wear to school."

"You bet I do. She chooses articles that were in style 50 years ago for her grandfather," said Lynn.

"I think you'll make a handsome grandfather someday," said Rachael. At that comment they all burst into laughter. Then Tony showed up with a strange look on his face.

"Am I that funny?" he asked.

"No, Rachael just said that she thought Lynn would make a handsome grandfather 50 years from now."

"You know," said Tony, "I think Rachael is right. I can just imagine Lynn with gray hair and a beard down to his waist hobbling along the street with his cane."

That comment began another round of laughter with more tears.

"If you people are finished laughing, I'll call my Mother and tell her to add some baby food to the crumpet mixture." Again all four of them laughed some more and then they walked down the street to the mall.

As they walked down the street, every so often one or more of the four would smile and chuckle a bit. The warm sunshine and light breeze made walking enjoyable, especially with friends.

"Have you chosen your classes for this semester? Lynn asked Tony.

"Yes, I am going to study English Literature, the History of England, Algebra II, and gym class. I think I'll try out for choir and an art class. At the mention of choir everyone stopped walking and looked at each other.

"Surely you jest," said Rachael. I've heard you try to sing and all you can do is growl."

"I've heard the school play involves a dog and I will make dog sounds. You know bark, growl, and wag my tail," said Tony, shaking his backside. Sara, Rachael, and Lynn could not walk any farther, they were laughing so hard.

"Tony, let's hear you bark and growl," said Lynn.

"Gr-r-r-r bark, bark" Then he walked over to Rachael and gave her a puppy kiss which was a lick on her cheek.

"Well, you have the barking down and the growling down good too, But I think you need to work on the puppy kiss," said Rachael. With that comment they all fell to laughing again holding their sides which began to ache.

"Tony, I didn't know you were such a comedian."

"If laughing makes a person fat, I think I've gained five pounds just today," said Rachael.

"Lynn, what courses will you study this semester, and no jokes this time?" said Sara.

"I think I'll study Physics, Spanish again, band, choir, Iowa history, maybe a cooking class, or a sewing class.

"Lynn, you cook?" asked Sara.

"Why not, if I develop skill as a cookie baker maybe we can open our own shop someday, unless you move away from River Valley after college," said Lynn.

"Hey, Lynn, are you going out for football this fall?" Tony asked, as they all strolled lazily down the sidewalk. Temperature was 95 degrees without a breeze to stir the leaves on the trees. They tried to stay in shade if possible.

Lynn turned to Tony. "Football is a sore subject at our house. My mom is strictly opposed to my playing, but my Dad says I have his permission to play. We talked about it earlier today. Mom is still opposed to the idea. She was in tears when I said I wanted to play this fall. She strictly forbade me to try out, She was afraid I'd be injured. Dad is in favor of the idea. Mom, of course, stamped her foot and shouted, "I thought we supported each other. I refuse to let him play that horrible and dangerous sport. The players purposely crash into each other, and then throw each other to the ground. It's like they want to injure their opponent." Her face hardened in anger.

I said, "Mom, I would be wearing a helmet to protect my head, plus shoulder and rib pads to protect my upper body, pads on my hips and legs to protect them."

"But those shoes have spikes on them."

"Mom, those are to help me run faster to get away from opponents who want to tackle me."

"I still do not want you to play football," said my mom. Dad, who had been listening silently, said "Go ahead with your school shopping. Your mother and I will discuss your playing football this fall."

"So I nodded and left the room," continued Lynn. "I paused by the door after closing it and heard an explosion: 'I am his mother! I

---

carried him for nine months and then raised him (with your help). I still refuse to give my permission for him to play that sport.'"

"My father answered in a calmer tone, but firm."

"And I am his father. I love you and I love him. You've made choices in the clothing he wears and who his friends are. He must learn to make decisions on his own. Maybe you want to choose his college and the girlfriend he will someday marry. He knows that choices have consequences along with benefits. He must learn to accept all of that when he makes a decision. He does an excellent job of choosing classes in school and friends. Sara is a wonderful girl. Tony has become a good friend since he became a Christian. So is Rachael. He did all of that without our help. I approve of all three of those people."

Lynn sighed. "With that, I left and didn't hear any more. But I'll talk to them some more after our shopping trip."

The four of them began walking again and soon arrived at the mall.

"Sara and Rachael, I want your advice on the shirts and slacks I choose today. I know nothing about style or fabrics," said Lynn.

"Sure, we'll be glad to help, on one condition: you stay out of the women's department. The articles we buy today require female knowledge and expertise," both girls said.

Both boys breathed a big sigh of relief.

"Is there a brand name that is in demand now like Old Navy and Ocean Pacific were a few years ago?" asked both Lynn and Tony. "We don't want anything with alcohol advertising or scantily clad girls or questionable scenes."

"Good choices guys," said Sara. "Let's see if there is a brand name we see often. Oh, here is a clerk. Maybe she can give us some suggestions." The clerk approached smiling and asked if she could help."

"Yes, we are shopping for school clothes and have no idea what other kids are buying." Is there a brand name that is in demand?" asked Lynn.

"There certainly is," replied the clerk with a big smile. "Just follow me." The clerk led them to the section of the store where shirts and shorts were displayed. "You'll find all kinds of Under Armor shirts and shorts in this section. Three aisles over there, you'll find The Buckle clothing for young men and ladies."

Sara and Rachael watched as Tony and Lynn searched through the shirts. "This is an ugly color," said Tony, as he returned a shirt to a stack of shirts. "Ah, now this color is really cool," he said as he picked up a sleeveless shirt in a bright blue color. "What do you think girls?"

"Hold it in front of yourself so we can see if it matches the color of your eyes, and if it goes well with your hair color," said Rachael with a wink at Sara.

Sara just smiled. "Smile so I can see the color of your eyes better. It goes well with your blond hair and is so close to matching your eyes. If you can find slacks in black or white you'll have an outfit. You'll have to be careful, Rachael, some other girl may try to snatch Tony away from you."

Everyone grinned and agreed the color made Tony look wonderful." Keep looking, Tony," said Lynn, "Maybe I can find something as cool as you found."

Lynn searched through the shirts and finally found a shirt with a mountain scene on the front. Holding it in front of himself, he asked in a serious voice, "What do you think girls?"

"The blue is close to your eye color. Will you let me change the color of your hair?" asked Sara as she smiled at Rachael.

"No" laughed Lynn, "changing hair color is for girls. In case you haven't noticed I'm a boy, not a girl."

"Oh, Lynn, you are a spoil sport," laughed Sara. "No, just kidding. I like you just as you are. Stay that way, my friend."

"Sara, you had me worried," said Lynn.

"What else will you search for Lynn?" asked Sara.

"A pair of shorts and some socks, maybe a pair of white socks and a couple of pair of black socks for dress up clothes."

Meanwhile Tony had found some shorts, socks, and another blue shirt supporting a baseball team.

"Why don't you girls go and look for your choices and we will meet you outside the Old Navy store in an hour," said Tony. "Is that long enough?"

"We will look here first and then go to Old Navy," said Rachael.

"Be sure to avoid any old sailors in Old Navy. They would be too old for you," laughed Lynn.

Sara and Rachael just smiled.

The boys wandered around the mall and played some games in the video arcade. After one hour they sat on a low wall outside of Old

----

Navy and waited. Soon Sara and Rachael walked out of the store each carrying a large bag with clothing articles.

"Did you find some cool clothing?" asked the boys.

"Yes, but you'll have to wait until we wear them to school. I'll show you one shirt."

Sara reached in the bag and pulled out a soft-colored yellow shirt.

"Hold it in front of yourself," said Lynn. "Oh Sara! That looks really nice with your brown hair and brown eyes. That may become my favorite shirt you wear."

"Rachael, what did you find?" asked Tony.

"Well, with my red hair, I thought green or black looks good. I like blue, also, but I get tired of black—it's so somber. I bought everything in blue shades, dark or light blue. Here are my choices: a sleeveless dark blue shirt, a three-quarter sleeve light blue shirt and a long-sleeved medium blue shirt. I figure I can sew some skirts to wear with them, so I also bought fabric."

"Looks like all of us made some good choices," they said together.

"Hmm," said Lynn. I see it is 3:30. I think my mother's tea party is over, so let's go clean up the leftover food."

"Grunt, groan, how will we ever haul all of this home"
complained the girls. "I wish I knew of a strong young man who would carry my bags." Sara and Rachael winked at each other and then bumped into Lynn and Tony.

Lynn said in a teasing voice, "Tony, do you know of a strong young man to help these damsels in distress?"

"No, I do not. I guess they'll just have to carry their own bags," teased Tony.

"You two young men are terrible, leaving us to carry our own heavy bags," said Sara. "If you want more cookies, Lynn, you'll help us."

"If you want to hold my hand---," said Rachael, looking at Tony.

"Lynn, old buddy, I guess we've been had by these fair young distressed maidens," said Tony.

"Yes, I guess so, but Sara, you only get one cookie at my house."

"Lynn, you are so cruel! Now I know why we are your only friends."

"Oh, all right, give me your bags and I'll carry them to your house for you."

Lynn took Sara's shopping bags and Tony took Rachael's. They all laughed with each other at their teasing, and commented about what good friends they had become.

Tony gently took hold of Rachael's hand and she smiled at him. "Gosh, thanks," said Tony. "I always wanted to hold your hand but was afraid you would slap my face if I tried." He gave her hand a gentle squeeze."

Rachael laughed. "You are such a tease."

Lynn and Sara just looked at each other and laughed too as they started down the street to Sara's home.

"Well, Tony, does holding Rachael's hand send shivers down your back bone?" asked Sara.

"Yes, it sure does, just tingles all over my body, but I think I could get used to this feeling. It's wonderful."

"Tony you are such a clown," said Rachael slapping his shoulder gently.

Upon arriving at Rachael's home, Tony gave her her bags and she smiled a thank you to him. "Thank you, Tony, that was kind of you to carry my heavy bags." Rachael carried the bags to her room, closed the door and told her mother she was going to Lynn's house with Sara and Tony and Lynn for an after shopping snack. When she walked out of her home, she walked up to Tony and took his hand in hers. Tony looked puzzled, until she said, "I told you if you carried my bags you could hold my hand" and she laughed. "Smile, big man. You've been my friend long enough so I give you permission. Just don't break it by squeezing too hard with your big muscles."

"I will be on my best behavior. Then taking her hand gently in his, he gave a slight squeeze.

"Ouch," said Rachael and then laughed. "You are such a teaser" she said with a big smile.

When they arrived at Sara's home, she took her bags from Lynn's hands. "Wait here on the porch and I'll be right back." She placed the bags on her bed and told her Mother, "I'm going to Lynn's home for some snack time with Lynn, Rachael, and Tony."

"Have fun Honey," said her mother.

Tony and Rachael walked ahead of Lynn and Sara.

"Sara, you must know I think you are a wonderful friend and I would never purposely hurt you in any way," said Lynn.

"Lynn, I am so grateful for the way you treat me and want what is best for me. You are a wonderful friend to me too."

"Would you think me too forward or bold if I asked if I could hold your hand?"

"Lynn I'm so glad you asked instead of forcing your hand into mine. I gladly give you the privilege of holding my hand. I trust you, Lynn."

"Thank you Sara."

Sara held out her hand, then giggled. Lynn's hands were full of packages. He could not hold her hand until Sara took one package from his right hand and held it so he could hold her left hand.

"Sara, this feels so good. I'll never take our friendship for granted. Soon

they reached Lynn's home and he led them all inside. All the older ladies were gone but there were two plates of cookies on the table with a note that said, "Kool-Aid is in the refrigerator."

"Go ahead and sit by the table, I'll take these packages upstairs. Tony wait until I come back before you attack the cookies.

"You're too late. He's already eaten three," said Rachael.

"They are good and delicious too" said Tony between bites of cookies.

"Rachael, take the plate from him, and Sara take the other plate, or we won't get any cookies," said Lynn laughing.

"Hurry up slowpoke. Shopping makes me hungry," Tony growled.

"Hold his hands, both of them Rachael, I'll be right down "

Lynn soon came down the stairs to find Sara with the plate of cookies on her lap, and one cookie in her mouth. Rachael had Tony's hands in a vice grip while he moaned about an empty stomach.

Rachael just smiled and refused to let go.

"Thank you ladies for saving some crumbs for me," smiled Lynn.

Sara took a cookie from her plate and said, "Lynn, open your mouth wide and close your eyes." Lynn complied and she gently placed two large cookies in his mouth and said "Now, chew!" Lynn smiled as his mouth ground up the cookies. Everyone laughed good-naturedly.

Lynn took a swallow of Kool-Aid and spoke. "I'm so glad we have all become friends and I pray our friendship lasts forever. Tony, since you and Rachael accepted Jesus as your Savior, you've become different people. Your attitudes have changed, your grades at school have improved greatly. Rachael, you are so pretty, too, with a smile on your face."

"Lynn and Sara we are so grateful you did not give up on us in spite of all the mean and nasty things we said and did to you. Thank you, most of all, for introducing us to Jesus Christ and helping us to accept Him as our Savior. Today has been fun and we're actually anxious for school to begin in two weeks."

Tony turned to Lynn and said, "I talked to the football coach and he gave me permission to help you learn how to kick extra pointers. Shall we start tomorrow?"

"I'd like that," said Lynn. "Shall we meet at 1:00 at the practice field behind the high school?"

"Yes," said Tony. They continued their 'tea party' and jocularity.

Lynn was a little subdued, though, knowing he needed to have more discussion with his parents about football.

That evening, Lynn asked his father: "Dad, may we discuss my playing football this fall after supper. We've got to convince mom that as the PAT kicker I'm not in as much danger as the linemen and the running backs."

"Do you really want to play football, Son?"

"Yes, and it will look good on my school record to have a sport rather than just academics. I think colleges want well-rounded students. I have band and choir on my record, but I think a sport would look good, too."

"All right, Lynn, but let's be gentle and soft-spoken no matter how your mother reacts.

Just then Marge's voice rang out from the dining room. "Ward and Lynn, supper is on the table, come before it gets cold."

"Okay honey, we will be right there."

"Oh Mom, something smells so good!"

Ward prayed, "Dear Heavenly Father, thank you for this food. Bless it to us and give us strength for our tasks. Bless she who prepared it and may we honor you. Amen."

Marge passed the roast beef to her husband, then the mashed potatoes and gravy, green beans and rolls. After they'd all filled their plates, Lynn said, "Mom, thank you for this delicious food." Dinner passed with pleasant conversation and afterward, Lynn and his father helped clear the table, put leftovers in the refrigerator, and helped Marge with the dishes and cleaning up the kitchen.

Afterwards, Ward said, "Come into the den, Marge. Lynn has something he wants to discuss with us." They each found comfortable seats, then Ward said, "Go ahead, Lynn."

"Dad, Mom, the position for the PAT kicker is open since that student graduated. I would go out on the field after River Valley scores a touchdown and attempt to earn an extra point by kicking the football through the goal post, then return to the sidelines. I'd hardly get dirty."

"I said no, and I mean no. I will not permit Lynn to play football," said Mother, looking at Ward.

With a determined look, Ward said, "I gave my son permission to try out for the sport and I hope he makes the team."

"I thought we agreed to support each other."

"He may not play forever, but football will look good on his high school record. When he goes to college he may not have time for a sport. That choice will be his to make alone."

"Are you just going to turn him loose to do as he chooses?"

"He is an intelligent young man. We cannot make his choices for him forever. He must stand on his own two feet. He will try out for the team with or without your permission."

"I will not go to his games and watch him play that horrible and rough sport."

"You may stay at home if you choose. But I will go to at least all of his home games, as well as some of his away games by myself if necessary, although I would rather you came along. If you do come along, you must be quiet when he is tackled, but cheer as loud as you can when he scores a touchdown, and weep no tears if he is slow to get up after he is tackled."

"Okay, I will yield to you as the head of our home and his father. I will pray the entire time of the game that God will protect him."

"So will I," said his father, who gave Lynn a hug before he went upstairs to bed.

Forever Hopeful

Chapter Fourteen

Lynn and Tony met the next day at the scheduled time. "I have five footballs in my bag so we don't have to chase a ball every time we kick one."

"Good idea."

"Lynn," said Tony, "We are going to run a lap today to begin to strengthen your legs. You need strong legs to be a PAT kicker so let's begin."

Tony began to run and Lynn tried to keep up but could not.

"Tony you run too fast, I can't keep up with you, slow down.

"Lynn, you need to keep up with me otherwise the ball will fall short of the goal post.

Lynn fell to the ground after the first lap.

"You're a tough coach, Tony."

"Tough coaches make champions. Do you want to be a champion or a failure?"

"If you put it that way, I want to be a champion," moaned Lynn.

"Good boy, Lynn, someday you'll thank me when they start to call you Mr. Automatic because you score every time. Now, we need some dry runs."

"Runs? You said one lap and now you talk about running again," moaned Lynn.

"Lynn," Tony laughed. "By dry runs I mean we'll practice the actual technique of approaching but there will be no ball. You'll just run up to the holder, which will be me, and swing your foot. I'll find fault with your performance."

"All right, coach. Let's begin."

Tony walked to the three yard line. "Do you see the short white line? That's where the officials will place the ball to be hiked to the holder. The linemen will line up to prevent the opposing team from getting close enough to block your kick and the backfield players will line up behind the linemen. Ten or fifteen yards from the short white line is where the holder will kneel to hold the ball." Lynn nodded his understanding.

"Football practice begins tomorrow," Tony added. "I'll introduce you to the coach and tell him what we did today. He'll watch you perform, offer some suggestion on your technique and style and decide whether you are on the team or not. Get a good night of sleep and eat a good breakfast tomorrow morning. I'll see you here in the gym tomorrow at 9:30 AM."

The next morning Tony and Lynn walked to the school house and found the head coach.

"Coach," said Tony proudly, this is Lynn Owens and he wants to play football this fall."

Coach Andrews looked at Lynn and asked, "Have you ever played football?"

"No sir," said Lynn with as much self-assurance as he could muster. "Tony said the position of PAT kicker was open since that player graduated last spring and I thought I could learn that position. Tony and I practiced for about two hours yesterday."

"How did you practice and what did you learn?"

"We ran one lap around the football field and then he explained the short white line in the middle of the three yard line as the place where the official places the ball to put it into play. He explained that the holder kneels at about the ten yard line and the kicker stands at about the thirteen or fifteen yard line about two or three steps to the holder's left, as I am right footed. At the call of hike, I start toward the ball and finally swing my right leg and just sweeping the top of the grass I kick the ball toward the goal post with the inside of my foot.

"That is all very good." Coach Andrews smiled.

"Thank you, Sir," said Lynn and Tony together.

"We did not use a ball yet, we just did some dry runs for about 40 times," said Tony.

"That is even better" said the coach. "Tony, here is a football, now both of you go to the equipment room and get fitted for a complete practice uniform and do 20 more dry runs and then start using the ball. I'll send the center out to hike the ball toward you. Start out in front of the goal post and after you've done 20 repetitions move to the right side and do 20 more and then move to the left side and do another 20. I'll be watching to see how you are doing and tell you about corrections if I see any to be made. Do another lap around the field before you practice kicking." Coach Andrews smiled and laughed, "You were hoping I'd forgotten that part didn't you?"

"Yes, Sir, we really did."

"Since you didn't moan and groan you need to do only one lap. The moaners and groaners get to do two."

"Thank you Sir."

Lynn and Tony collected their practice uniforms from the equipment room, carried them to the locker room, and changed their clothing. Once dressed, they moved out to the practice field and began to run their lap.

"I always wondered how football players could run with all these pads and other things on their bodies, but it isn't so heavy once you grow accustomed to it. It's just like it's not there," observed Lynn.

"It is there to help and protect you, not to hinder you." said Tony.

Both boys jogged around the field at a comfortable rate of speed and then went to the end of the field where they met the center.

"Hi, Tony and Lynn," said Frank. "We've got to work together on this and become like a well-oiled machine. Let's talk about what you expect from me and what I expect from you. You expect I will accurately hike the ball to you Tony, and you, Lynn, will start toward the ball as soon as you hear hike and see the ball flying through the air to Tony. If my hike is correct, Tony will have it on the tee as your foot comes forward to kick the ball through the uprights."

"Let's do some dry runs." Frank ran to the ball on the three-yard line and Tony knelt about seven yards behind him. Lynn backed up from Tony three steps, and then moved two and one half feet to the left. At the word "hike," Lynn started toward Tony and when he

---

arrived where Tony knelt, Lynn swung his foot. His cleats caught in the grass, so he missed the ball.

"Yesterday, while we were practicing, I didn't have cleats on. I'll have to adjust my foot up about an inch," said Lynn.

"Let's do it again," said Frank.

This time Lynn swung his foot without catching his cleats in the grass. Tony had jerked the ball up. "I didn't want to chase the ball," he said.

The boys continued to practice until they had done twenty repetitions. Then they kicked the ball. The first kick went to the left, the second to the right. "It's supposed to go straight through the uprights," said Lynn. What am I doing wrong?"

"You are not holding your foot stiff," said Frank. "You are letting your foot flop around. Try holding it stiff like you hold it when you are placing your foot on the ground when you are walking. After you kick the ball you can flex your ankle."

"Let's try again," encouraged Frank.

This time when Lynn's foot met the ball it flew upward at a good angle and flew straight through the goal posts. "Look at that pig skin fly!" said Tony, slapping Lynn on the back.

"Let's do it again," said Frank, "Try for two in a row, Lynn."

Frank hiked the ball, Tony held it on the tee and Lynn kicked it again. "Bulls' eye" shouted Tony. Frank smiled. The boys completed 20 required kicks then moved to the left. Except for a few mistakes Lynn made the proper adjustments and then they moved to the right side of the goal post. This time there were fewer errors.

After all the repetitions, the coach approached and said "Tomorrow we will try you under fire, Lynn. Some of the team will charge and try to block your kicks."

"I'll do the best I can, sir," said Lynn.

"Just call me Coach."

Lynn dreamed that night that sometimes his kick flew right over the heads of the charging players, and at other times the kick was low enough that the players could block the ball.

Next morning at breakfast Lynn's mother said, "Lynn I do not like you playing football. The sport is too rough; I do not want to see you hurt."

"Mom, I've told you about all the pads and the helmet I will wear. The rules are that the other players can't touch me under a ten yard penalty. Why don't you come to practice for a little while today and watch what I do during the game?"

"No! I will not go and watch other players run into my son on purpose!"

"Mom, you just do not understand how the game is played and what the rules are for playing."

This time she stamped her foot and shouted, "I will not watch my son get hurt playing that foolish game." After saying that, she ran from the kitchen to her room, slammed the door shut, and threw herself across the bed crying. Lynn quietly left the house and went to football practice.

He quickly dressed in his football gear and ran out to the practice field, picked up a football and tee, and began to kick the ball through the goal posts.

"Players, gather round me," said the coach. "Here's what we are going to practice today. Running backs, I have five new plays for you. Defensive players will practice tackling the opposition so they fumble the ball. Also, see if you can block the kicks for PAT. Go to your assigned end of the field. Lynn and Tony, go to the north end, and defensive players, too. All others to the south end. Let's see some improvement in your performance today. Improvement means no laps at the end of practice. No improvement means everybody runs three laps on the track. I'll count the laps."

Lynn and Tony ran to the north end of the field and Tony bent down on one knee and laid the kicking tee in the grass. Lynn backed up three steps and moved two steps to the left of Tony.

"Should I cut back on the number of steps?" Lynn asked Tony.

"No, Lynn. That should be fine. We can adjust if we see we need to make changes."

They heard the voice of the coach: "Defensive players, line up on the two yard line; offensive players on the four yard line facing each other. Tony and Lynn you are in proper position. Now you know what to do. Defense you will try to get through the offense to block the kick. Offense you will block the defense to keep them from getting through. If you run into the kicker you will run an extra lap. Now let's do it. Quarterback, call the signals and Tony, shout "hike" on the third hut. Any questions? Let's do it."

Every one took their positions. The quarterback called "hut, hut, hut," and Tony shouted "hike." The ball came flying back to Tony and as soon as Tony said "hike," Lynn began his approach to the ball. Swinging his foot, the ball flew off the tee and over the heads of the rushing players. The ball flew through the uprights and the coach blew his whistle.

"Tony, good job of setting the ball on the tee. Good kick, Lynn. Defense, you were kind of slow. Do it again."

The players took their positions again and the quarterback said "hut, hut, hut." Tony said "hike" and Lynn ran to kick the ball. Again it sailed high over the heads of the defense.

"Defense, I need to see you block a kick. You must be faster and jump higher. Do it again."

After ten more attempts the defensive players finally blocked a kick.

Whew! I sure am tired, thought Lynn. *I'll have to run more now so I don't tire so quickly.*

"Lynn, come by me. I want to talk to you."

"I'm on my way coach; what do you want to talk to me about?"

"I'm glad you tried out for football this fall, and I wish you had played all three years in high school. I've watched you practice with Tony while I was in my office. You've learned to be a PAT kicker quickly. We needed a kicker since our previous kicker graduated this past spring so I welcome you to the team." The coach smiled and clapped him on the back. "Continue to come to practice. I'm putting you on the weight machine to strengthen your legs and you'll do more than PATs. You'll do kickoffs and punts too."

Lynn smiled and said, "Thank you, Coach, for your praise and confidence in me. I'll try not to let you down, nor the team. I'll go to the weight room right now and spend 15 minutes on the machine.

"No more than 15 minutes, Lynn. I don't want you injured before the season starts. After a week you can increase the time to 20 minutes and up the weights too, we'll talk about the amount of weight later."

Forever Hopeful

Chapter Fifteen

The next morning Lynn awoke at the usual time. "Lynn," called his mother. "Get up. We need to register you for school today.

"I'm already up and about dressed. Sara and I are going together to register for classes."

"Come down and eat your breakfast."

Lynn arrived in the kitchen and sat down to a breakfast of scrambled eggs, bacon, and toast with a tall glass of orange juice.

"Jeepers, Mom, this tastes really great. I could smell the delicious odor upstairs in my room."

"Thank you, Lynn. Now what is this about you and Sara going together to register for classes? And what subjects will you study this fall?"

"I think I'll sign up for basket weaving, photography 1 and 2, cooking, art and voice lessons."

"Lynn what has gotten into you?"

"Mom, I'm just teasing you. I'm really going to study Physics, European history, trigonometry, an art class, and choir."

"That sounds better than basket weaving, photography and cooking. What about gym class and band?"

"I'm out for football so I do not need to take gym class. I'll think about band but I can't play during games because of football."

Lynn cleaned his plate and put down his fork. "I'm going to Sara's house now to pick her up and we'll walk to the school."

"I'm going, too," said his mom.

"Mom, I can handle it by myself. Just stop by school later and pay the fees." Lynn smiled with a wave as he walked out the door."

 Mother leaned out the door. "But Lynn I've always gone with you."

"Mom, I can handle it by myself. Do your knitting or something. I'll be home for lunch." He quickly walked away.

Marge flopped down on a nearby chair. *That boy has become impossible, I used to do everything with him and now since he met Sara, he would rather be with her. I don't understand what has cau* *this change in him.*At that thought, the doorbell rang and a friend entered the house.

"Oh, Sybil, I'm glad to see you. I have a question to ask you. I'll get you a cup of tea first."

"That would be lovely," Sybil said, with a smile. "Could it be iced tea? The weather is so warm, I am wet all over from walking the block from my house to your house."

"Sure, I'll make some iced tea for you. I have a gallon jar on the back deck for sun tea."

As they seated themselves at the table, Sybil said, "You have a question to ask me?"

"Yes. I've always gone to school with my son, Lynn, and registered him for classes. This morning he told me he could handle it by himself and he was going with his friend, Sara. Then he laughed and said good bye as he left the house."

"That Sara Brown is such a lovely girl, said Sybil.

"I know she is and so pretty, too, but he seems to want to do things with her instead of with me," said Marge.

"I can't blame him," said Sybil. "He has discovered girls and I saw them walking down the street last week holding hands."

"What?" Marge's mouth was wide open in shock.

"I said they were holding hands," said Sybil.

"He didn't talk to me about doing that!"

"I think you can trust Lynn and Sara."

"Sybil, he needs to discuss these things with me. I'm his mother. He should talk to me about his decisions."

"Oh Marge, I suppose you want him to ask for your permission to kiss her someday, and another day to become engaged and later to marry her."

"Yes, I do, Sybil, I have his best interests at heart."

"Marge, let him grow up and make some decisions on his own. Has he ever made a foolish decision or embarrassed you by what he has done? Last year at registration I overheard the principal say that if everyone were like Lynn they wouldn't have any problems."

"I'm his mother and I have the right to know what he is doing and what his plans are..."

"Marge, he needs to live his own life. If you insist on controlling his life, you'll lose him when he moves as far away from you as possible.

"Do you think so?"

"Yes, Marge. He has already started with the football thing, and holding Sara's hand. Stop trying to rule his life. You think about what I've said."

Marge, by this time, was sobbing uncontrollably.

Sybil stood up and said, "Thank you for the iced tea. I'm leaving now.

Sybil quietly left the house. Marge continued to cry and went to her room, closing the door.

Meanwhile, Lynn walked down the street to Sara's home, singing to himself. Soon he arrived at the Brown's home and rang the doorbell.

Sara answered the bell. "Hi Lynn. I'm ready to go to school and register for classes." They started down the street. "What classes are you going to take?"

"I'm taking Physics, European History, Trigonometry, an art class, and choir. What about you Sara? What classes will you study?"

"Well, I'm leaning toward a sewing class, Physics, Trigonometry, European History, gym and maybe American Literature."

"Now that you mention literature class, I may take one too. We'll be able to study together after football practice and on Saturdays at the public library."

"Oh, Lynn, I'd look forward to that---- like we used to do the last couple of years."

"I enjoy being with you, Sara."

"I enjoy being with you, too, Lynn."

"Sara, may I hold your hand as we walk to school?"

"Lynn, I give you my permission to hold my hand any time we are together. You don't have to ask each time."

"Thank you." Lynn gently took her hand in his hand. Sara smiled up at him. Lynn had all he could do not to shout with joy.

Soon they arrived at school and entered the gym to register for classes.

"Good choices, kids," said the counselor. "Both of you are seniors this year and always choose good classes and earn excellent grades. But Lynn, what about gym class? It is not among your choices."

"I'm playing football this fall, so I don't have to take gym. The coach asked me to come out and Tony helped me learn to be a place kicker."

"Well good for you. I know you'll do well."

"Thank you. My mom will be along later to pay the fees."

As they left the building, Lynn smiled at Sara and asked her, "May I take you to the Dairy Queen and buy an ice cream cone for you?"

"Why Lynn, are you asking me for a date?"

Lynn stopped walking, turned toward Sara and said, "Yes, I am. Don't you think it's about time?"

"I would be proud to give you permission to take me to the Dairy Queen for ice cream. I'll even let you hold my hand while we enjoy the cones and conversation," said Sara.

"Young lady, I thought you would turn me down," teased Lynn. "Let's hurry before you change your mind."

"There's no way I'd change my mind with ice cream involved."

With that she took his hand and looked tenderly into his eye. "Let's go, big boy. I'm hungry."

"Now let's settle this question: What flavor of ice cream is your favorite: vanilla, chocolate, or strawberry?"

"I like all three the best. Just order two cones of the same flavor."

"Oh Sara, we are so alike and enjoy so many of the same things we are starting to think alike. I want to surprise you at Christmas time and really surprise you. Make a list of possible Christmas gifts for me to choose from. Alright? I'll do the same and let's agree on a price range and not spend more."

"Excellent idea. I am thinking under $30.00."

"I agree. But we will not ask each other for the amount we spent."

"Good rules. Here we are at the ice cream shop."

Forever Hopeful

Chapter Sixteen

On Monday morning, Tony showed up at Lynn's front door. "Well, Tony, you are here early."

"Yes, we need to go to the high school and get familiar with the weight machine and then kick some more PATs."

"All right, I'll be ready to go in about a minute. I'm anxious to get on the weight machine and strengthen my legs. I want to impress the entire school and all the people in town," sad Lynn.

"You've a goal in mind and we have a week before school starts to gain some strength. Then we have a week before our first game, so we should be close to ready. We'll make a good combination and score a lot of points," said Tony.

"My mom finally gave in and, while she will not come to the games, I have her reluctant permission to play football."

Lynn and Tony walked to the high school and dressed for practice. Soon other members of the team came and dressed, too.

"Hi guys," said Tony. "Let's have a good season and try to go undefeated. Maybe we can win the conference championship."

"That would be a first," said Robbie, a linesman.

"We'll never do it if we don't have a goal and strive to reach it," said Tony."

"What is Lynn doing here?" asked Robbie.

"I'm here to kick PATs."

"I thought you were all brains and no brawn. It seems like you always have your nose in a text book."

"I often do," said Lynn." Robbie, maybe I can change your opinion of me. I always wanted to play football."

"From what I've seen so far this summer you've already begun to change my opinion of you." Robbie smiled and gave Lynn a high five.

Soon Tony and Lynn were finished with the weight machine and perspiration was dripping from Lynn's chin. "I hurt now, Tony, but you know the old saying: "No pain, no gain.""

"You were supposed to stop before the pain began, Lynn."

"The coach said fifteen minutes and then stop, so that's what I did. Tomorrow I'll stop after 10 minutes. Then, the next day I'll try for 15 minutes again. I would like to get up to 30 minutes on the weight machine, if coach approves," said Lynn.

"Go to the water fountain and take a drink, then rest a little while. Then we'll do some dry runs by the goal post," said Tony. "I think after about 20 dry runs coach will send some players to try and block a few of your PATs.

Lynn and Tony sat on a bench and watched the rest of the team go through their plays and drills.

Soon some mothers and high school girls came to watch the rest of the practice. "There are Sara and Rachael in the bleachers," Tony said. Lynn started to stand up but Tony pulled him back down.

"I just want to say hello to the girls."

"We can talk to them after practice, but now we need to concentrate on football and not on girls," said Tony.

"Spoil sport," said Lynn.

"You can hug Sara and thank her for coming after practice. Now we concentrate on football. Concentration and practice are part of winning games. Girls are for after games and practice."

"Yes, sir, slave driver," said Lynn, with a laugh. Tony and Lynn went to the end of the field and practiced more PATs.

After practice Lynn and Tony walked over to where Rachael and Sara were sitting.

"My goodness but you two fellows don't smell very good right now," said Rachael. "What do you think, Sara?"

"I agree."

"Do you have any suggestions for improvement?" asked Tony.

"If there was a lake nearby we would toss both of you in and let you soak for a while," said Sara laughing.

"Do you think you could, and still stay dry?" asked Lynn. Sara loved how his eyes twinkled.

Sara simply laughed and said, "You wouldn't dare."

"You are right" said Lynn. "I think too much of you to ruin that pretty dress you are wearing. Why don't you find a shady spot or go into the school house library while we shower and then we can all go to my house and see if my mom has some lemonade and cookies."

"I'm glad practice is over for today. And I am thirsty for some lemonade," said Tony.

After their showers, Lynn and Tony found the girls in the library.

"You young men certainly smell better," said both girls.

"Well, since we smell better, may we hold your hands as we walk to Lynn's home?" asked Tony.

"Of course you may," said Rachael. "Lynn already has hold of Sara's hand."

"Sara and I came to an agreement about hand holding." Lynn grinned at them. "She told me I didn't need to ask any more but I was welcome to hold her hand any time we were together and I would always have her permission."

Lynn smiled at Sara as they walked to his home. Along the way, they discussed what they thought classes would be like and how difficult they would be. "There will be many lessons on math, and on science, electricity, and mechanics to name a few topics. In literature we will read much ancient writing and poetry. Band and choir we already know about from last year. Sara, may I ask why you are taking a sewing class?"

"I looked at how much money I spent on clothing at the mall. If I learn how to sew I will be able to make my clothes and spend about half as much money. If I learn to sew well enough I may sew a shirt for you and maybe I'll make a matching pair of shorts for us.

"That would be cool to have matching shorts."

"In the class on trigonometry we will study the properties of triangles, different kinds of triangles, and finding unknown angles. With all that information in our brains we will probably walk stooped over when we walk." Both Lynn and Sara laughed. "You'll look like a grandma and I'll look like a grandpa. We will be so busy we won't have time to get into trouble."

Lynn's face got serious. "Seriously, Sara, I don't want us to get into any kind of trouble. So let's make a promise to each other that

----

we will respect each other and not do or say anything disrespectful about or to each other, always speaking the truth about each other."

Sara nodded.

A few days later, Lynn and Sara sat on the front porch of Sara's home. "Sara, we've had a good summer and have had some good discussions. Now it's time for school to begin. I've noticed that, sometimes in school, boys and their girlfriends have pet names for each other, and I'd like to do that. I have no objection to your name, but I've thought about the pet name, Sweetie. It's not a put down, but a name that expresses how I feel about you. You are such a sweet girl and always so sweet and kind to me. I can think of no other name that fits you better. What do you think?"

Sara smiled. "That's okay."

"Does a name for me come to your mind?"

"Lynn, I have always liked your name, but you have always been my hero so that is what I will call you."

"Sara, I appreciate that you treat me with respect. I will always try to be the gentleman you deserve." Sara smiled and squeezed his hand.

School began and with it new classes and fall sports. Soon the first game on the school calendar of the football season was upon them.

The head official of the game handed the ball to Lynn and trotted to the side line. At the proper time he signaled to Lynn to kick the ball. Lynn approached the ball and, swinging his right foot, lofted the ball toward the opposite goal post.

Players from both sides ran toward the ball but only one player tried to catch the ball and run with it. Lynn kept his eye on the player who caught the ball as Sara cheered in the stands and shouted "Good play, Lynn, and good tackle."

On the first play from scrimmage, the ball carrier fumbled the hand off and Tony recovered the ball. River Valley owned the football on the 15 yard line.

The play called was a short pass over the line, complete to a running back from River Valley. That player ran with the ball into the end zone. The score of the game was now River Valley 6, opponent 0. Lynn came back onto the field. Tony slapped Lynn on the shoulder. The center hiked the football. Lynn kicked the football through the uprights. Sara cheered and clapped her hands for Lynn.

The official handed the ball to Lynn and he placed it on the tee.

As Lynn approached the ball, the crowd cheered and stamped their feet. Again the ball flew through the air to the end zone and was caught; that opponent was immediately tackled. The coach took Lynn out of the game. "Good job Lynn."

The two teams moved the ball down the field. The first quarter ended with the score 7 to 0 in favor of River Valley. As the teams changed sides of the field, they smiled to each other. The parents and friends of the players on both sides clapped and cheered. Sara and Rachael were all smiles as Tony and Lynn ran to the River Valley bench and sat down to drink a small cup of water.

Tony smiled and looked at Lynn. "I heard the opponents talking about River Valley's new kicker: They said, "Who is that kicker? Did he just move to River Valley?"

"No," the other fellow said. "He has gone to school there since kindergarten."

"Maybe we can break his big toe so he can't kick PATs and field goals."

"Be quiet! Coach will hear you and you'll be off the team. You know how he is about fair play. If we are going to win I want it to be honestly."

Tony explained to Lynn, "There is a new rule about targeting an opposing player. The penalty is the ball is placed where the targeting occurred, the player is removed from the game to the locker room and the offender is not allowed for the rest of the game nor the next 3 games. We need to block our opponent in the proper way, without breaking the rules of the game."

"I also heard our opponent say, "We've got to keep River Valley out of the end zone because TD is worth 7 points. We also need to keep him outside the 35 yard line. He can kick a 35 yard field goal with no problem. Two field goals are worth one touchdown." So I guess they are impressed by you."

With the start of the second quarter both teams settled down to play football and win the game. Neither team wanted to fail their fans but River Valley had the better, more skilled players. By half time the score was 21 to 7 in favor of River Valley. During the break, River Valley was feeling proud of themselves and their performance. The coach pulled out some of the more skilled players to give those with less skill a chance to learn. They won that game.

River Valley High School celebrated this first victory with a lively dance supported with local musicians. Everyone was happy and danced with enthusiasm and much joy. The principal said, "Students and team, your conduct was praiseworthy. And team let's have more successful games in the rest of the season."

Forever Hopeful

Chapter Seventeen

The next opponent was not known for their football skills, but River Valley prepared as if they were the conference champions the previous year. Lynn practiced each day kicking PATs and improved his skills, plus those involved with punting. This strengthened his legs.

During the game, River Valley scored at will and won by a score

of 56 to 0.The record now stood at 2 wins 0 losses. Lynn successfully kicked 8 PATs. The students began to call Lynn Mr. Automatic, much to Lynn's embarrassment. He said, "I'd rather you called me Lynn, but the credit for helping me to be a PAT kicker goes to Tony, my coach."

The third game went well, also.

Meanwhile, Lynn and Sara continued to study together and learned about European History as well as Trigonometry or Trig, as they called it, the study of triangles and their properties. The school choir began to prepare for a Christmas concert. A lot of time was spent on "What Child Is This," "Sleigh Ride," and "Rudolph the Red Nosed Reindeer."

European History covered the Dark Ages. "I'm glad I didn't live

then "said, Sara. "Nobody learned anything new, how boring. Life sounded so strange. People did not travel, girls could not learn at school. All they could do was cook at home, sew, marry early and be almost a servant in their home,"

Tony added, "The boys had some privileges, but at a very young age they had to learn a trade."

Tony, Rachael, Lynn, and Sara kept diligently at their school work. They spent much time studying for their classes in order to maintain good grade averages. All four of them enjoyed school and wanted to earn excellent grades.

The third football game was more of a contest since both schools had equally talented players. River Valley won by a score of 21 to 14. Lynn had a successful kick after each touchdown. With a lead of 21 to7, the players no longer played to score but to keep their opponent from scoring.

Lynn continued to learn about football and being a PAT kicker. Each week his reputation grew. One newspaper interviewed him, but he gave credit for his skills as a kicker to Tony and his team Coach.

Their Coach introduced two exotic plays that were used in the fourth game and produced two Touchdowns.

The last game of the season found everyone in River Valley in high spirits since the school was undefeated in the football season. The stadium was full of people, cheering and talking as the game began. Play ragged back and forth on the field. In the fourth quarter River Valley recovered a fumble and scored a TD. Their coach signaled Lynn to kick the PAT so Lynn pulled on his helmet and ran onto the field. The quarterback called the count and the ball was hiked to Tony, the holder. Both lines exploded into action, bodies fell everywhere. Lynn approached the ball and swung his foot making contact. As the ball headed toward the goal post, a huge lineman from the opposite team crashed into Lynn. They both fell to the ground. A large crack was heard and Lynn's right arm bent at an unusual angle. Lynn lay on the turf and it seemed he could not get up. Tony ran up

----

to Lynn and looked at his friend. Lynn said, "Buddy, ask the coach to come out here, I think my arm is broken."

The coach came and, after his examination, signaled for the paramedics who confirmed the coach's opinion that Lynn had a broken arm. The paramedics splinted Lynn's arm and loaded him into the ambulance. The opposing player was removed from the game and a targeting penalty was called. The ball had gone through the uprights so River Valley now led by 28 to 7.

Lynn's Dad placed his arm around Sara's shoulder and said, "Let's go to the hospital so we can see Lynn. They may not have his arm set yet but we can ask for more information about his condition."

"Yes, let's do that," said Sara, through her tears. Upon arriving at the emergency room desk, the nurse asked who they were and they told her they were Lynn's father and Lynn's girlfriend. The nurse at the desk smiled and said, "Did he get hit by a truck or what?"

"No, a large lineman ran into him while he kicked a PAT. We could hear the bone break in the bleachers."

"Ouch! You may wait in the emergency room waiting area until the doctor comes and tells you that you may see him."

Sara and Mr. Owens sat down to wait until the doctor came. The doctor explained, "The break was a simple break and there are no other injuries. But he can't play football for a while. He is sleeping soundly and will be sedated through the night, so you might as well go home and see him in the morning."

Lynn's father turned to Sara, "So I suppose you'll make another box of cookies for Lynn?"

"Of course." Sara smiled at him. "But if you continue being such a nice gentleman, I'll make a box for you, too." Tears glistened in her eyes.

Lynn's father patted her shoulder sympathetically and reassured her, "Lynn will be all right. Thanks for being such a good friend to him. He thinks the world of you."

Lynn's dad took Sara home and then went to his own home. His wife opened the door immediately and asked, "Where's Lynn?

"He was injured by a large line man from the opposing team. He has a broken arm. The doctor put a cast on it. He decided to keep him at the hospital overnight for observation just to make sure there are no other injuries besides the broken arm. They'll release him in the morning. Sara is making cookies for him. Be nice to her."

Lynn's mother began to cry and wail loudly. "I knew this would happen, and it's all your fault." she screamed. She continued for an hour after which Lynn's father said, "I'm going to bed."

"How can you sleep with our son in the hospital? I should go there and make sure he is all right."

"The nurses will care for him, that's what they are trained to do."

"I still want to go to my son."

"Stay at home. "You'll just be in the way so they can't care for him."

"Don't you care about him?"

"Yes, I do, but it's only a broken bone."

"How can you be so cruel?"

"I'm not cruel." Ward said sternly. "I realize Lynn is injured, but there is nothing I can do for him at the hospital. The doctors and nurses are trained to do that, like I said. We will just be in their way so they can't care for him."

His wife just stared at him while she continued to cry uncontrollably.

Finally Lynn's dad raised his hands in disgust and said, "I'm going to bed. We'll go and see him in the morning and bring him home."

When Lynn's mother saw Lynn the next morning, she broke into tears again.

The nurse in the room just said, "He's going to be all right. The break wasn't that serious. He is in good physical condition and that will help him heal sooner."

"Thank you" said Lynn's father.

At that moment, the doctor walked into the room and said, "You must be the parents of this young man. What a fine young man he is. The break in his arm was a clean break and should heal quickly. I suggest no more football this fall. I'd like to see him again in two weeks to see how his arm is healing. Until then, Lynn, do nothing more strenuous than holding your girlfriend's hand." Then he winked at Lynn and Sara and left the room.

Sara looked at Lynn and smiled. Then she said to Lynn's dad and mom, "I'll help keep him on the path to returned health. The doctor did not say we could not study together."

"I'll even help carry your school materials and type your papers for you, Lynn. You'll be better in no time and then you can carry my books for me again." Lynn smiled at her.

"Dad," said Lynn, "What was the final score?"

"At the end of the game the score was 30 to 24 in favor of River Valley."

Lynn pumped his unbroken arm. "Great!"

Sara looked at Ward and Marge, "Now, how about some cookies at my parent's home?"

Forever Hopeful

Chapter Eighteen

On Monday, Lynn went to school and sat in his usual seat. His friends and class mates gathered around him and congratulated him on a good season and wanted to sign his cast. "You may," Lynn said, "but you'll have to wait for Sara to sign first."

At noon, Lynn and Sara met for lunch. They planned to study at the public library after school, then walk to Sara's home for cookies. Sara signed Lynn's cast with her nick name, "Sweetie," and Lynn's nick name: "My Hero."

The school year passed quickly. When graduation was only one month away, an assembly was held to recognize those who had earned honors during the school year and in all their high school years. Tony was recognized as the most improved student. Rachael was on the honor roll. Lynn and Sara were recognized as co-valedictorians of their class with A grades in all their classes.

They both applied and were accepted to be students at Pere Marquette University in River Valley. Lynn would major in history and Sara in nursing. They studied hard and the years went fast.

In their final year of college, Lynn decided it was time for a change. "Mom and Dad, I'm going to Sara's house to talk with her. I hardly get to see her since we enrolled in college. I'll be home in about an hour from now." Mounting his bicycle he peddled to Sara's house. Once there he rang the doorbell and was soon admitted to the house.

"Come inside Lynn. We are always glad to see you."

"Is Sara at home?"

"Yes, she is in the dining room studying. Pick a spot on the couch and be comfortable, I'll tell her you are here."

"Thank you, sir.

Soon Sara and her Dad reappeared in the living room. Sara smiled as soon as she saw Lynn. "What brings you here this time of night?"

"I want to talk to you about something that is on my mind. May we go back to the dining room to have our conversation? Then after we complete our talk you can tell your parents what we discussed."

Lynn and Sara returned to the dining room. The smile disappeared from Sara's face when she saw Lynn's expression. "Lynn you look so serious. Are you ill?"

"No Sara, nothing like that. I do have a serious question to ask you."

Sara began to cry. "Lynn are you tired of our relationship and don't want to be my friend from now on?"

"Absolutely not, Sara, but my question and your answer will determine our future."

"Please explain this to me. I'm confused."

"Sara, I have kept a special place in my heart just for you. You are a wonderful girl and a true treasure to me. I fell in love with you at our youth group meeting and hay ride. Love for you has only grown stronger over time." Taking Sara's hand, he knelt on one knee and said, "Sara, will you give me the honor and privilege of marrying me and becoming my wife?"

Sara put her hand on her mouth and just stared at Lynn. When she could finally speak she hugged Lynn and said, "Yes, yes, a thousand

---

times yes. I will marry you." They kissed, and then Sara said, "Come we must tell Mom and Dad."

Lynn smiled and said, "May I place this on your finger first?"

"Ohh, it's beautiful!"

Upon entering the living room, Sara said, "Dad and Mom, Lynn just asked me to marry him. Do you approve of my answer of yes?"

"Of course we approve!"

Lynn smiled. "Now I can sleep tonight. I was afraid you might say 'no' to my proposal. May I stop by tomorrow and walk to school with you?"

"Of course you may, My Hero."

"Who is My Hero?" asked her mom.

"It's my pet name for Lynn because he is always encouraging me."

"Sometime we need to get together with my parents to choose a date for the wedding and all the details. I have some ideas right now, but Sara may not like some of them. We need to make decisions," said Lynn.

"Tell me your ideas now and I'll say 'yes' or 'no' to each one." said Sara.

"Okay. For best man I choose Tony...

"And I choose Rachael for Maid of Honor," said Sara.

"For organist, how about Brenda?"

They continued discussing wedding plans for the rest of the evening with stars in their eyes.